Dear reader,

You've received this book for free because it contains some printing errors. Instead of discarding flawed copies, I'm sharing them with book lovers like you who value the joy of reading.

Though this book isn't perfect, its stories still hold value and I hope they'll inspire you. If you enjoy the read, you can help more readers find it by leaving a review on Amazon or another online bookstore.

Happy reading, and thank you for giving this book a new home.
Stefanie

Woven by War

*A Team's Experience of
Russia's War in Ukraine*

Dr. Stefanie King

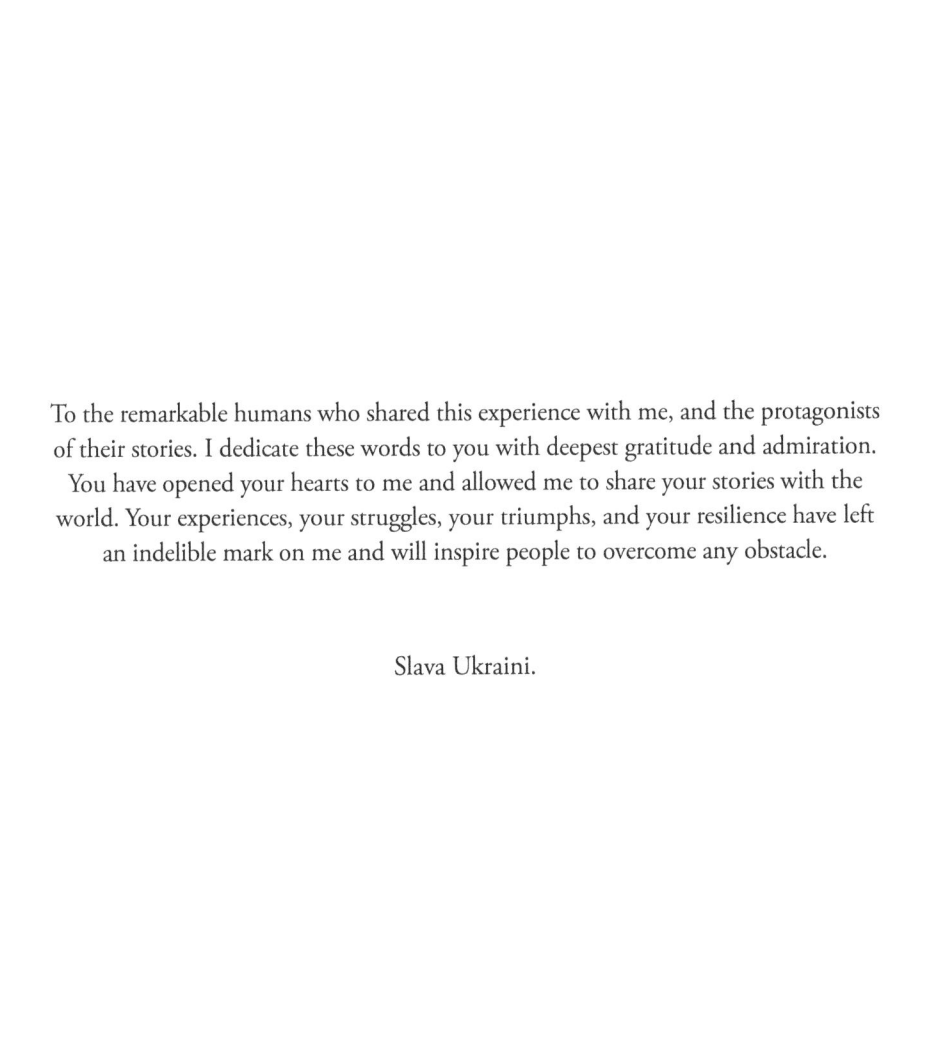

To the remarkable humans who shared this experience with me, and the protagonists of their stories. I dedicate these words to you with deepest gratitude and admiration. You have opened your hearts to me and allowed me to share your stories with the world. Your experiences, your struggles, your triumphs, and your resilience have left an indelible mark on me and will inspire people to overcome any obstacle.

Slava Ukraini.

Contents

Preface...ix
Dramatis Personae..xiii
A brief timeline of Ukraine's history..................................xvii

Chapter 1 - On hope and premonitions..............................1
Chapter 2 - The day time froze..5
Chapter 3 - One light, many shadows................................13
Chapter 4 - Deep in the tunnel...19
Chapter 5 - Stay or run?..23
Chapter 6 - Wrestling with the grind.................................27
Chapter 7 - And then he laughs...31
Chapter 8 - Vodka, love, and sacrifice................................37
Chapter 9 - We are all Ukrainians.....................................49
Chapter 10 - A new home..53
Chapter 11 - Trapped..57
Chapter 12 - No good time for a holiday..........................61
Chapter 13 - Yet again, cancelled.......................................65
Chapter 14 - Everything matters..67
Chapter 15 - One hell of a Monday...................................77
Chapter 16 - Tides of fear and reverence...........................81
Chapter 17 - Lviv, you've changed.....................................93
Chapter 18 - A race against time......................................105

Chapter 19 - My home, near the front line..111
Chapter 20 - A journey into the unknown...117
Chapter 21 - Sheltered, yet adrift..125
Chapter 22 - Storms and bad omens..135
Chapter 23 - The guilt of the lucky..141
Chapter 24 - Erase my language, erode my identity....................................145
Chapter 25 - The burden of injustice...149
Chapter 26 - Together, we'd be strong..153
Chapter 27 - Who are we? The quest for restoration...................................157
Chapter 28 - Grasping for the new normal..161

Epilogue...165
Acknowledgements...171
Photographic Credits..173
About the author...174

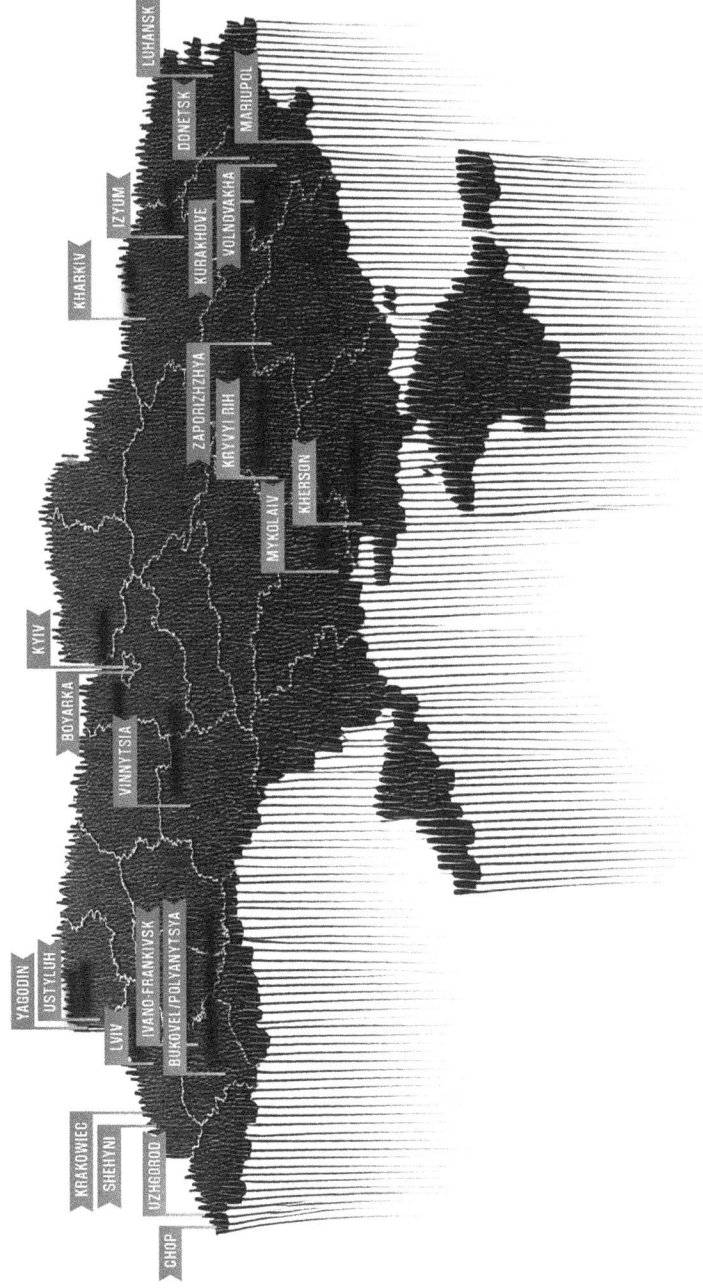

Preface

By Stefanie King

Sydney, 6 April 2022. It is early morning, and I find myself awake in my bed in Australia, jet-lagged. It has been forty-one days since Russia invaded Ukraine. As has become my routine, my first thoughts are of my former colleagues. Their stories and images haunt me. Driven by an urge I have not felt since my teenage years, I rise and start writing about my experiences during the first days of the war.

Having a blank page in front of me feels like a heart-to-heart conversation with myself. As the words flow from my heart to the paper, writing becomes my refuge, a patient listener to memories I have not shared with anyone. Releasing these thoughts brings relief. Confusing flashbacks suddenly gain context and meaning, and buried emotions find an outlet.

I did not intend to write a book or document any specific aspect of the war. I simply wanted to record my experiences. For months, I kept it to myself. When I eventually shared that I was writing with my former colleagues, I was surprised that they volunteered to have me document their stories, too. Throughout 2022 and 2023, I collected stories from women and men, Ukrainians and internationals, current and former colleagues, each recounting their version of 24 February 2022.

Before diving into these incredible stories, dear reader, allow me to explain the origins of this book. In February 2022, I worked for a company primarily employing Ukrainians. Contrary to what you might expect, we were completely unprepared for the invasion. On the morning of 24 February, I became part of an ad hoc task force with three others—two Ukrainians and a German—to support our colleagues in the war zone as best we could. Russia's attack turned their lives upside down, and how they navigated the turmoil was both heartbreaking and inspiring. Parents drove for days in their desperation to bring their children to safety, couples hugged each other one last time at the border unsure if they would reunite, and children found their own ways to understand the war, forever shaped by its impact on their families and country. They all faced difficult decisions: should they flee their homeland or stay? Should they leave their loved ones behind or stay with them? Should they fight in the army or support its efforts from a distance?

Their stories never started with them; rather, they originated with previous generations. Most of us remember 24 February 2022 as the start of this conflict, but it dates back to the eighteenth century, when the Russian Empire annexed the region east of the Dnipro, incorporating it into what is now Ukraine. Ukrainians have since endured many horrors: massacres, oppression, and persecution. The Soviet government caused the Holodomor in 1932–1933, a man-made famine that killed over seven million people, recognised as genocide by the EU and US Congress. In an attempt to Russify the Ukrainian people, the use and study of the Ukrainian language was forbidden for decades.

Despite these trials, Ukrainians continued to fall in love, start families, build cities, and live their lives to the fullest. What strikes me most about every single Ukrainian I talked to is their resilience, hope, and ability to remember that there is life beyond war, even in the face of death. My first thought when they told me their stories was that they deserved to be heard.

Reliving these memories is incredibly painful, especially as the war continues. The intense emotions they navigate daily—fear, despair, anger, sadness, joy, hope, and love—are palpable. Some individuals chose to remain anonymous, asking for their names to be changed to protect their identities. Others were initially enthusiastic about sharing their experiences but later found the process too draining and withdrew. Some stories are partly fictionalised to fill in the gaps where memories were too painful to revisit.

The characters in this book include developers, engineers, designers, teachers, electricians, and public servants, ranging from four to fifty-four years old. An anthropologist or sociologist would rightly point out that they do not represent the diversity of Ukraine's ethnicities, religions, cultures, and sociological backgrounds. This is because the characters are part of a young company focused on building digital products.

Writing these stories was an incredibly challenging experience. Each one is precious to me, and I strived to do them justice through empathetic interviewing, thorough research, and writing to the best of my abilities. I am acutely aware that I am neither Ukrainian nor have I experienced this war firsthand. No matter how hard I try, I can never fully comprehend the pain of witnessing one's country being invaded, the strength required to defend it against all odds, and the ineffable sacrifices this entails. Therefore, I ask you, dear reader, to approach this book with an open heart.

The stories in this book aim to shed light on the daily struggles of Ukrainians, and many others worldwide whose lives have been upended by forces beyond their control. In the following pages, you will discover moments of tenderness mixed with sorrow, hope amidst tears, and courage prevailing over fear. This is Ukraine since February 24, 2022.

I hope this book will inspire you to stand by Ukraine in its fight for justice, understanding that this war ultimately concerns us all.

Dramatis Personae

IN ORDER OF APPEARANCE

Danylo   *1990, Ukrainian.
Head of Design.
Location on 24 February 2022: Delft, Netherlands.

Larissa   *1993, German.
Program and Operations Manager.
Location on 24 February 2022: Münster, Germany.

Olena   *1986, Ukrainian.
Marketing Manager.
Location on 24 February 2022: Düsseldorf, Germany.

Dmytro   *1987, Ukrainian.
Olena's husband.
Location on 24 February 2022: Düsseldorf, Germany.

Sophia   *2018, Ukrainian.
Olena and Dmytro's daughter.
Location on 24 February 2022: Düsseldorf, Germany.

Serhiy   *1990, Ukrainian.
Developer.
Location on 24 February 2022: Lviv, Ukraine.

Vlad   *1992, Ukrainian.
Serhiy's brother.
Location on 24 February 2022: Lviv, Ukraine.

Vitalii *1994, Ukrainian.
DevOps engineer.
Location on 24 February 2022: Kryvyi Rih, Ukraine.

Diana *1994, Ukrainian.
Vitalii's wife.
Location on 24 February 2022: Kryvyi Rih, Ukraine.

Natalyia, Anastasia, Andriy
Ukrainian.
Vitalii and Natalyia's children.
Location on 24 February 2022: Kryvyi Rih, Ukraine.

Svetlana *1989, Russian.
Operations Manager.
Location on 24 February 2022: Münster, Germany.

Farid *1989, German.
UX Researcher.
Location on 24 February 2022: Lviv, Ukraine.

Iurii, Victor, Daria, Mati, Lesya
Ukrainian
Farid's friends
Location on 24 February 2022: Lviv, Ukraine

Iryna *1968, Ukrainian
Public servant; sister of one of our clients
Location on 24 February 2022: Boyarka, Ukraine

Anastasiia *1997, Ukrainian.
Data Engineer; Bogdan's wife.
Location on 24 February 2022: Münster, Ukraine.

Bogdan	*1996, Ukrainian. Technical Lead; Anastasiia's husband. Location on 24 February 2022: Münster, Ukraine.
Natalia	Ukrainian. Anastasiia's mother. Location on 24 February 2022: Kharkiv, Ukraine.
Ivan	Ukrainian. Anastasiia's father. Location on 24 February 2022: Kharkiv, Ukraine.
Lesya	*2002, Ukrainian. UX/UI Designer. Location on 24 February 2022: Mykolaiv, Ukraine.
Ludmila	*1985, Ukrainian. Teacher; Lesya's mother. Location on 24 February 2022: Mykolaiv, Ukraine.
Petro	*1981, Ukrainian. Electrician; Lesya's father. Location on 24 February 2022: Mykolaiv, Ukraine.
Stef	*1988, Austrian-Australian. Partner Venture Building and Accelerator Programs Location on 24 February 2022: Berlin, Germany

Dramatis Personae

A brief timeline of Ukraine's history

9th-13th Centuries – Kyivan Rus

Formation of Kyivan Rus, a medieval state that laid the foundation for Ukrainian, Belarusian, and Russian identities. It was a major power in Eastern Europe before its decline due to internal conflict and the Mongol invasions in the 13th century.

14th-17th Centuries – Foreign Rule and Polish-Lithuanian Commonwealth

After the fall of Kyivan Rus, Ukrainian lands became fragmented and were dominated by neighboring powers like Lithuania and Poland. Ukraine was incorporated into the Polish-Lithuanian Commonwealth, which led to periods of subjugation and influence by foreign rule.

1648-1657 – Cossack Hetmanate

Under Bohdan Khmelnytsky, the Cossack uprising against Polish rule established the semi-autonomous Cossack Hetmanate. This era is seen as a key moment in the development of Ukrainian self-determination and national identity.

Late 18th Century – Division by Empires

After the collapse of the Hetmanate, Ukraine was divided between the Russian Empire and the Austro-Hungarian Empire. The southern and eastern parts of Ukraine were under Russian control, while the western regions were ruled by Austria-Hungary.

19th Century – Cultural Renaissance

Despite political subjugation, Ukraine experienced cultural revivals, with intellectuals fostering a sense of national identity through literature, language, and history.

1917-1921 – Struggles for Independence

Following the collapse of the Russian Empire during the Russian Revolution, Ukraine briefly declared independence. A period of intense fighting between various factions, including Bolsheviks, nationalists, and foreign powers, followed, eventually leading to Soviet control.

1922-1991 – Soviet Rule

Ukraine became part of the Soviet Union. This period was marked by the devastating Holodomor (1932-1933), a man-made famine, Stalinist purges, and the suppression of Ukrainian culture and language.

1939-1945 – World War II

Ukraine was a major battleground during World War II, suffering enormous destruction and loss of life. More than five million Ukrainians died fighting Nazi Germany.

1986 – Chernobyl Disaster

The explosion at the Chernobyl nuclear power plant in northern Ukraine had far-reaching environmental, health, and political consequences.

1991 – Independence

With the collapse of the Soviet Union, Ukraine declared independence in 1991. This marked a significant turning point in its modern history.

2004 – Orange Revolution

Following widespread protests against electoral fraud, the Orange Revolution led to a re-run of Ukraine's presidential election and the victory of pro-Western candidate Viktor Yushchenko.

2013 – Euromaidan and Russian Annexation of Crimea

The Euromaidan protests in Kyiv, sparked by the government's refusal to sign an association agreement with the European Union, culminated in the removal of President Yanukovych. Shortly after, Russia annexed Crimea and conflict erupted in Eastern Ukraine.

2019 – Ukraine's New President

Volodymyr Zelensky won the presidential election run-off in a landslide victory over incumbent Petro Poroshenko.

2022 – Russia's Invasion

On 24 February, 2022, Russia launched a full-scale invasion of Ukraine.

Chapter 1

On hope and premonitions

23 February 2022

I enjoy starting my days with BBC's Global News Podcast. Unbeknownst to the broadcaster, they have been my steadfast companion since September 2013. The podcast is published twice a day on weekdays and daily on weekends. I like the morning routine and dependability. Every morning, as I rise from bed, I open Spotify on my way to the bathroom and play the latest episode. While I brush my teeth, I place my phone on the bathroom cabinet and absorb the first news of the world that has unfolded while I was asleep. It is always the same presenter. Thank you for being a reliable companion, Jackie. I wonder how many people's bathroom tiles her voice echoes from every morning. I usually catch the headlines while applying toothpaste before Jackie's voice gradually fades into a background murmur, drowned out by the steady vibration of my electric toothbrush. By the time I brew my morning coffee, Jackie has moved on to the special news report of the day. 'Russia's invasion is becoming increasingly likely,' she says, 'US information suggests Putin is preparing to invade a democratic country.' I sense worry and urgency in her voice. Although her reporting remains professional, it is evident that she is well aware of the weight her words carry, the weight of concern, the weight of the unimaginable, and the weight of the world teetering at the brink of a third world war.

It is February 2022, and Berlin is engulfed in the depths of winter. The snow has settled on the windowsills, coated the trees in a pristine white, and covered the streets with a dreary amalgamation of ice and mud. As I adjust the heater, my thoughts drift towards Ukraine and what its people might be preparing for at this very moment. Another woman in her mid-thirties in Kyiv might well be listening intently to Jackie's reports on the threat looming over her own country. Hopefully, they would be better informed than I am, more confident about the scenarios that this situation might turn into, more resolute in their response to them, armed with answers while I seem to have only questions. I contemplate how I would ready myself for a possible invasion of my home by one of the world's biggest military forces. Would I choose to stay or flee? Would my family be willing to come with me? Which loved ones would I worry about the most? I ponder what possessions I would gather and what I would leave behind. I am wondering a lot these days. My father always praised me for having both feet firmly on the ground and keeping a clear head rather than being in the clouds. I was never one to ruminate or lose myself in thought, yet my mind seems uncontrollable these days. Glancing at the clock, I realise I am running late for work. I tell myself to stop worrying about uncertainties and focus on my first meeting, which I need to be ready for in less than thirty minutes.

Our leadership team call on 23 February is different. As a remote team, we dial in from several different cities across Germany, the Netherlands, and Ukraine. The company was founded during the COVID-19 lockdown in 2020 with the mission to build digital products that make a positive impact on the world. Like any startup, life is equally exciting and chaotic. With a team of nearly one hundred individuals, we continue to create rules, rhythms, and processes as we need them. We keep things light and enjoy our playful banter. However, today is different. A heavy sense of unease permeates the air. The one you feel when you enter a room where people have just had a heated argument. Attempted jokes elicit a brief giggle at best before they drown in awkward silence. For the first time in our weekly calls' history, there is only one item on the agenda: Ukraine, Russia, and Putin.

'I believe we need a business continuity plan. We need clear actions and responsibilities for the different scenarios that might be coming our way.' I say. 'Especially for the worst one,' I almost whisper now. Contrary to what some may claim, saying it out loud does not make it more tangible; instead, it just makes it more surreal. It is reassuring that everyone else seems less worried than me.

Sadly, Ukraine has endured multiple invasions throughout its history. If Russia follows through on its threats, the eastern parts will be most affected. Our office is in Lviv, Ukraine's westernmost metropolis, which has a population of approximately 800,000, which we believe is not a primary target for Russia. However, our status as a remote-first company allows our employees to work from anywhere. Some of them live in Kyiv, Kharkiv, and other cities in Ukraine's east. In response to the situation, we already started searching for twenty short-term apartments in western Ukraine and Poland two days ago. We will offer them to any team members who wish to relocate. Our plan for the worst-case scenario involves relocating all employees to Germany, where our official headquarters are located. Yesterday, we contacted Germany's immigration office to enquire about work permits for refugees and the necessary preparations as an employer. As there is no official emergency plan in place, we were told all staff members would have to follow the standard procedure. This entails individually approaching the German embassy in Kyiv and applying for a blue card, with a waiting time of ninety days for the appointment and a processing time of up to one month for the visa.

On today's call, we agree to provide assistance for relocation to employees residing in cities at the highest risk of being targeted by Russia, and to complete a business continuity plan this week. The plan I am drafting this evening reads like a block of Swiss cheese, with lots of yellow marks for placeholders and gaps we will hopefully fill in the coming days. I head to bed praying this plan will never see the day of execution.

Little did I know that the world would look so different the next morning.

Chapter 2

The day time froze

24 February 2022

It happened. They did it. This is bad. What scares me most is that I have no idea how bad. I replay BBC's Global News Podcast, carefully listening to Nick's report once again. The information regarding Russia's invasion is scarce.

I think back to the stories that my grandfather told me about World War II. The brotherhood within the army. The uncomfortable uniform never fit him and itched in the most unpleasant places. The longing for food, water, and shelter after hours in the trenches. His desperate attempt to warm up his fingers that had frozen stiff on the rifle. The screams that pierced the night when a comrade fell to a bullet or wrestled with the haunting images of the day in his dreams. The suffering of women and children on the streets. The emptiness in their eyes, their sunken cheeks, pale skin, and thinning hair from months of cold and hunger. The unintended casualties. The stench of rotten flesh from soldiers hastily left behind with no time for proper burials, let alone funerals. The fear of never seeing his loved ones again, of dying alone and namelessly on the next battlefield.

I briefly curse my sheltered upbringing in Austria, which has left me ill-prepared for this reality. What foolishness. What privilege. My knowledge is confined to films, history books, and the fragmented stories my grandfather shared when the red wine that he loved so much triggered memories and swept away all inhibitions. I scramble to recall any facts and figures from these limited sources that might help me form a mental image of the current situation in Ukraine.

It is just before 8am, and I repeatedly remind myself not to succumb to panic. I get dressed and make my way to my usual spot in the coworking space in Berlin Mitte. A glance at my inbox leaves no doubt that we have all seen the news and are bracing for something bigger. Most of today's meetings have been cancelled without explanation. With a sense of urgency, I leave a message in our leadership channel on Slack: 'Bad news overnight. Let me know how I can help. I'm ready to roll up my sleeves and support in any way needed.'

As the clock strikes 10am, there is no response. I proceed with the few scheduled calls that have not been cancelled, but everything we discuss feels trivial. My mind is scattered and I find myself distracted, wondering what the world looks like for the 44 million Ukrainians who woke up to the same news or, worse yet, experienced the invasion firsthand in the early hours of the day.

Around 1pm, Danylo, our Head of Design, reacts to my message. 'We have started a call to discuss what needs to be done. Jump on.', he says.

He is a Ukrainian based in Delft, a small town south of The Hague where cobblestone streets wind through charming canals. With his dark brown hair cropped short and his moustache and beard neatly trimmed, he is sitting at a large desk in his home office. Behind his transparent-framed glasses with black earpieces, one can glimpse a mischievous spark in his green eyes, which twinkle when matching his infectious chuckle before the punchline of a joke. We got along instantaneously when we first met last year, and our shared appreciation for a well-crafted pun strengthened our bond. He is a playful soul, balancing light-heartedness with complexity in character, and creativity with practicality in his approach to work. Without knowing it, he brings levity to my life, for a long day filled with meetings never feels quite as hard when he is there.

Danylo forwards me the link to the video call, a Google Meet link ending in 'pjt-ymcz-uhx'. I know the combination of letters by heart to this day. It strikes me that we have never used Google Meet before this moment. As a startup still grappling with financial constraints, a Zoom subscription is one of the few luxuries we have granted ourselves. Five other people are already on the call, engaged in a discussion about the number of employees affected and the necessary measures to assist them. Our most pressing concern is arranging buses to evacuate our employees to Poland and ensure their safe passage to Germany. I offer to contact the Polish embassy to inquire about their stance on accepting Ukrainian refugees. As Ukraine is not part of the European Union, its citizens typically require a travel visa, with a waiting period of several days. However, Poland has reacted swiftly in response to the crisis. While their papers will still be checked at border crossings, Ukrainians are granted immediate entry to Poland as refugees.

The distance from eastern Ukraine to our humble company headquarters in Germany, which consists of two rooms we rented cheaply from one of our investors, equals a gruelling twenty-six-hour drive. We are unsure about the condition our employees will arrive in and how many will choose to accept our offer to help them escape the war zone in the first place.

Halfway through my call with the first bus-hiring company I could find on Google, I realise that I am sitting in a bustling coworking space in one of Berlin's busiest neighbourhoods. I am surrounded by more than a dozen individuals who are eagerly typing away on their laptops, nodding in sync with the music playing through their headphones, or engaging in a conversation with their co-workers. For a moment, I am frozen, taking in the focused hustle around me. They all seem engrossed in their tasks, seemingly oblivious to the extraordinary tragedy unfolding today. However, the nature of the conversations I am about to partake in is far from suitable for a public setting. I hastily gather my scattered belongings from my desk and rush out the door. While the tyres of my old bicycle clatter over Berlin's merciless cobblestones, I call my partner to let him know that I am heading home and that our planned weekend getaway to Amsterdam will likely need to be cancelled. In my haste, I forget to lock my bike and take two steps at a time as I make my way up the four flights of stairs to our apartment. I catch my breath and unload the contents of my backpack onto our working desk. Without delay, I reconnect to the video conference call.

At any given time, there are four of us on the call, with a few others intermittently joining to offer assistance in any way they can. We assign the tasks on the list we created and mute ourselves while we are on the phone with embassies, rental companies, concerned clients, and hotels. We could easily disconnect and reconvene later, but there is a sense of reassurance in knowing that none of us is in this alone and that we might somehow make it through this crisis together.

My research progresses slowly and grindingly. I do not speak Polish, Ukrainian, or Russian, and my English is of little use. The best I can do is conduct research on border crossings from Ukraine to Poland. I squint, trying to memorise the names of the towns I encounter. I gauge distances between them on Google Maps to identify the most viable escape routes. My usually reliable memory keeps failing me, making me repeatedly check the same information. We expect the majority of our employees and their families to cross the border at Shehyni-Medyka, and then transit in Krakow before continuing their journey to Germany.

By 8pm, we have finalised the initial evacuation plan. The first group of employees will be transported out of Ukraine by bus via the Shehyni-Medyka border crossing, and will be accommodated in Krakow for one night before embarking on the second leg of their strenuous drive to Germany, a country unfamiliar to most of them. Larissa, our Venture Program Lead, has located a hotel in Krakow. The twenty-nine-year-old German has gone about the task with the determination and practicality we are used to from working with her. Her previous internship as an international travel reporter has given her adept research skills and a maturity that seems to surpass her years. She often wears her light brown hair in a casual high ponytail, with a few cascading strands framing her winning smile and clear brown eyes. They sparkle when she recounts stories of her trip around the world and the friendships she forged on her travels. Behind those eyes dwells a kind spirit that thirsts for exploration and adventure. Clad in a comfortable yet stylish blue crewneck jumper, she blends the resilience of a seasoned adventurer with a strong sense of dependability. She confidently tucks a loose strand behind her right ear as she explains the details of the accommodation agreement.

The owner of the hotel has generously offered to reserve the entire hotel exclusively for our team while only charging us for the rooms we will use. He has even agreed to personally drive to the border and pick people up in his car. We are immensely grateful for this offer. We are a start-up, still in debt, barely making ends meet, and by now acutely aware that relocating over eighty people and their families at such short notice will require every resource available to us.

Time has become a strange and fluid concept by now. We are messaging our employees who are online, listening to news updates, and joining groups on a messaging platform called Telegram to make sense of the situation in different cities across Ukraine. The majority of our employees have sought refuge in basements, shelters, or bunkers, bringing with them whoever and whatever they could in the few minutes they had to leave their homes. The minutes following reports of new waves of bombings feel like hours, the hours between them like minutes. All over the world people are holding their breaths with us as bombs rain from the sky. They destroy streets, houses, fields, and farms, set homes in Kyiv and Kharkiv on fire, and wound whatever is within their radius of indiscriminate destruction.

The journey for our employees making their way from eastern Ukraine towards the Polish border will be arduous and fraught with challenges. They will have to travel across the country on congested streets and overcrowded trains. Despite the relatively short distance of less than ninety-five kilometres between Lviv, where our office is located, and the Shehyni-Medyka border crossing, it will likely take days for them to reach their destination. We anticipate that around thirty employees located in western Ukraine will cross the border tonight and reach Germany within the next forty-eight hours. We all stay on the call till midnight and agree to take turns so that we can support anyone who might need help throughout the night. As I head to bed at 2am for a few hours of sleep, I leave Danylo to take on the night shift until 5am, when he will hand the reins to Olena.

Olena joined the company in March 2021, the same month I did. The teacher-turned-marketer and mother of two wears her long golden-brown hair down most days. While her days are filled with the sweet chaos of parenthood, she navigates her work responsibilities in the most structured manner. In the few interactions we have had until now, I have been captivated by both her gentle nature and the steadfast resolve she emanates. Her emerald green eyes are a mirror of her emotions, often glimmering with curiosity and kindness, and roaming the room when she is solving a tricky problem. Tonight, they look exhausted, lined with the weight of worry and restlessness.

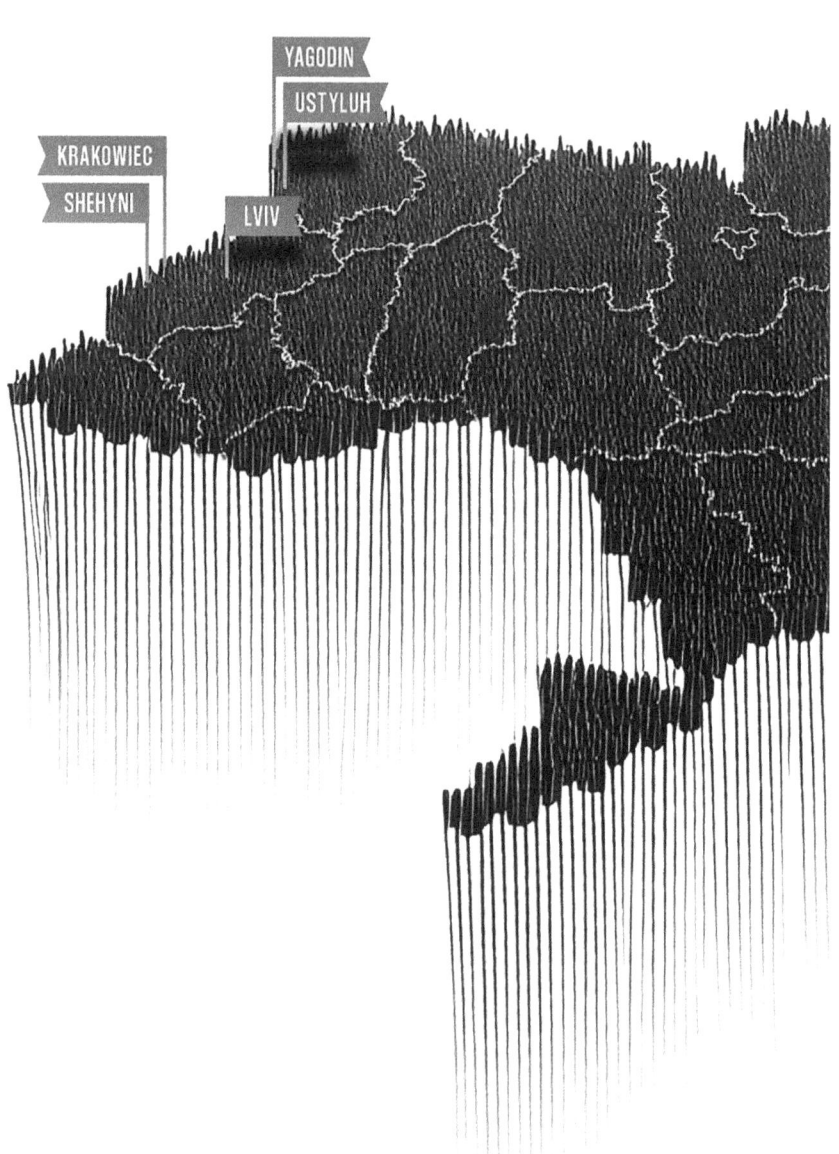

Chapter 3

One light, many shadows

25 February 2022

By 6am the next morning, I am wide awake and heading straight to my laptop on the work desk in the living room. The call disconnected when it went to sleep mode. As I refresh the tab in my Chrome browser and rejoin, Google Meet announces my reappearance with the distinctive chime that indicates a participant's arrival in the meeting. Bing. Olena turns on her video and mutters a tired, 'Good morning, Stef.' Together with her husband Dmytro, she has taken over the early morning shift from Danylo at 5am, diligently carrying out the tasks at hand despite the exhaustion that lingers in her voice.

Working remotely from our homes for almost two years due to the ongoing COVID-19 pandemic has allowed us to catch glimpses of each other's private lives. We have witnessed the occasional interruptions by children introducing themselves to their parents' 'new friends', dogs chasing balls across apartments, and partners tiptoeing about in the background with fresh loads of laundry. For many of us, working from home has revealed life in its most forthright reality. The boundaries between work and our personal lives have blurred, and we have come to accept the challenges of juggling both simultaneously.

However, as I softly respond, 'Good morning. How are you?', to Olena in my pyjamas, I realise that this is a new level of bareness. Today, we are united in the rawness of this morning, marked by shock, grief, and a sense of profound empathy after a day and night filled with terrifying reports of shelling across Ukraine. As our weary eyes and pale faces stare back at each other through the screens, I feel more connected to her than ever.

The morning shift is grim. Bomb shelling intensified in the early morning, during people's most vulnerable hours of the day. While I was asleep, missiles were raining down upon the country, launched from hundreds of kilometres away, far from the devastating suffering they have inflicted on the ground. Ukraine is on the front page of all newspapers today. The headlines paint a harrowing picture of the tragic losses on the first day of Russia's invasion. 137 Ukrainian soldiers and civilians were killed, and hundreds more wounded. The reports from courageous local journalists are soul-stirring to read and the haunting video footage sends shivers down my spine. Reporters call it a 'Blitzkrieg'. They believe it will be a matter of days until Russia declares its victory and absorbs Ukraine into its territory. The odds seem insurmountable, with Russia's sheer size and military strength dwarfing Ukraine's. It is a battle between David and Goliath. For us, it means that we have no time to lose.

Our communication channels with them fell eerily quiet overnight, leaving us suspended between hope and despair, uncertain of how to interpret the silence. In the depths of bomb shelters, access to cell phone reception is often unreliable, and many wisely choose to conserve battery on their phones, aware that the next opportunity to charge them might be hours away. Then, finally, there is a sign of life, and it comes with uplifting news from Krakow. According to the latest reports, over 50,000 people have fled Ukraine by now. Among them were our developer Serhiy and his brother.

Like us, he woke up to yesterday's news about the invasion, and swiftly packed his belongings without a second thought. While throwing the essentials into his black duffel bag, Serhiy called his brother Vlad. There was no time to reflect, consult the family, or discuss the best course of action. The brothers stopped at their parents' home for a fleeting farewell and rushed to Shehiny. The checkpoint was fairly crowded but not yet overwhelmed by demand. They reached the border well before the convoy of vehicles waiting to cross it into Poland. Serhiy took a deep breath and stroked his clean-shaven head, a gesture he often made when feeling stressed or overwhelmed. The border guard briefly scanned their documents, exchanged a few words with them, and gave them a telling look as he ushered them through. He knew that Serhiy was one of the last men he inspected before martial law would restrict further departures.

Upon crossing the border, the brothers were warmly received by Polish volunteers handing out sliced meat sandwiches, herbal tea, and bottled water. They held up hastily crafted signs with information about buses and trains destined for various cities in Poland. Despite wearing gloves, their hands trembled in the biting cold of this merciless winter day. Serhiy and Vlad boarded one of the crowded buses headed for Krakow. The large vehicle, typically employed for inter-city travel within Poland, provided space for over fifty seats. The 260-kilometre drive to their destination seemed to pass by in a blur. For the first time since they had woken up, they caught their breaths and reflected on what they had just gone through. The weariness from the long and eventful day began to take its toll as the bus dropped them off in the heart of the city, a mere hundred metres from the hotel we had arranged for them. They were grateful to arrive, and in desperate need of rest before they could continue the second leg of their trip to Germany.

As Serhiy lay down on his bed, the magnitude of his decisions and impressions of the day sank in. The expressions of sadness and compassion he had witnessed on the faces of the volunteers at the border. The awareness that his possessions now amounted to nothing more than a single duffel bag resting at the foot end of his bed. Flashbacks of people and places surfaced, reminding him of all the beautiful things he had left behind. It was painful to think of the loved ones he had left behind to save his life. In an effort to find calm, he took a deep breath and glanced over at Vlad, who lay in the second bed next to his. He was awake, too, and staring at the ceiling. They began the day as proud Ukrainians, two independent men in their late twenties, filled with dreams and aspirations at the prime of their lives. As they crossed the border to Poland, a new, weighty label was thrust upon them: refugees. A marker for people far from home. People in a foreign country. People who had no choice but to rely on the mercy and kindness of others for their very survival.

Less than four hours after Serhiy and Vlad crossed the border, Ukraine's President, Volodymyr Zelenskyy, declared martial law. A strict prohibition was placed on Ukrainian men aged eighteen to sixty, banning them from leaving the country, with borders heavily guarded by Ukraine's watchful State Border Guard Service.

It is now 6.30am, and the distinct sound of 'Bing' notifies us of Larissa joining the call. Our morning is consumed by relentless research as we delve into accommodation options on both sides of the border. Hotels, holiday homes, and bed and breakfast places are filling swiftly, with people seeking refuge close to the border, anxiously awaiting their chance to cross. More and more cars are lining up at all border crossings to Poland and Romania. The convoy of vehicles at Shehyni stretches over more than eight kilometres by now. By the end of the day, it will swell to a staggering forty kilometres.

Seventy per cent of our employees based in Ukraine are males. With President Zelenskyy's decision to enforce martial law, our plans to evacuate them to Germany have been dashed abruptly. Our focus now shifts to an equally critical and daunting task. We need to determine how many of them would be willing to entrust us with the evacuation of their families and how we can support them while they themselves are prohibited from leaving the country. While President Zelenskyy has yet to summon every Ukrainian male to take up arms, the looming possibility weighs heavily upon us.

One person dominates my thoughts. Theo, who is in his mid-thirties, is one of our talented user experience designers. Based in the vibrant city of Lviv, he became part of our company in June 2021, initially joining as a freelancer to work on a product development project that I led. He has a gentle yet resolute nature, rarely engaging in conversation but displaying ingenuity when he does choose to speak up. While his work was consistently exceptional, I sensed a certain ambivalence for the first few weeks of our collaboration, as if he did not enjoy it much. I struggled to make sense of his straight face but was determined to win him over. Secretly, I embarked on a personal mission to elicit at least one genuine smile from him whenever we spoke.

After three months, we made him an offer to join the company as a permanent employee. To my surprise, he accepted under one condition: that he would continue working alongside me. With this revelation, he shattered my previous confidence in reading people easily, and taught me about the danger of interpreting the cues of others through our limited lens. He illuminated the myriad ways in which human connection can manifest itself, for which I was so grateful. Day by day, smile by smile, we slowly formed a bond.

The mere thought of Theo being summoned to bear arms makes my heart recoil. I am unsure if he has completed Ukraine's mandatory military service, ever wielded a gun, occupied a trench, or experienced the claustrophobic interior of a tank. I try to suppress the thought that many of our people would face grim odds if they had to enter the front lines of this war. If you had the choice between saving your life and defending your country, which would you pick? How much is a life worth in the struggle for the survival of an entire nation? How much is it worth when democracy itself is at stake? The choice between protecting our own lives and defending our country is one we cannot fathom until we are forced to do so. We do not know how our employees feel about this decision, and it is not ours to make. The best we can do from our distant desks, hundreds of kilometres away, is to provide them with viable options.

I switch to satellite view on Google Maps, zooming in on the border between Ukraine and Poland. If it bears any resemblance to the border of Austria and Germany, where I grew up, there may be hidden crossing points. Abandoned tracks in the forest perhaps, where a vehicle can be concealed and one can cross by foot, or small river crossings located far from official checkpoints and vigilant border guards. Our research yields a few potential routes that appear feasible, and we carefully mark them on the map, each with detailed notes on our findings that we will share with our team in Ukraine.

Chapter 4

Deep in the tunnel

25 February 2022

On the second day of this invasion, there is no end in sight to what many had predicted to be an unavoidable annexation within a matter of days. Ukrainians continue to pour across the borders into Poland and Romania, seeking refuge from a war that they did not choose and escaping to an insecure future. A significant number of them will select Germany as their destination, hoping to find safety and support. However, there has been no official statement from national, federal, or local authorities regarding the infrastructure that will be in place to assist these refugees.

Our best plan for the moment is to relocate our employees to the city of Muenster in Germany where we have several staff members and a small office space. A popular student city, its population fluctuates throughout the year with students arriving for university studies and returning to their hometowns during holidays. As students are on break in February and March, we are exploring the option of renting dormitory rooms for the first few weeks of our employees' arrival. Affordable apartments and hotels are scarce and would require more time and funds to secure than we have available. As a service company, our workforce is the primary source of revenue, and the sudden collapse of operations has significantly impacted our financial stability. Despite these challenges, we are committed to continuing to pay wages to our employees for as long as possible, regardless of their ability to work.

I initially assumed that every company with ties to Ukraine or Russia would find itself in a similar state of concern until I learned that this was far from accurate. Our clients and business partners were surprised to learn that our efforts extended beyond mere prayers and donations.

While our immediate focus is on the short-term challenges that the chaos of this war throws at us minute by minute, we are well aware that we must quickly develop strategies to pivot our business model. With our current reliance on labour arbitrage, shifting our workforce from Ukraine to Germany and adjusting salaries accordingly will undoubtedly lead us down a path towards insolvency.

I am deeply immersed in this thought when my partner opens the door to the living room and announces that dinner is ready. I take a seat at the table but find myself distracted and struggling to focus on the plate in front of me. My ears remain attuned to any sounds from my laptop in the next room. I have muted myself but remained connected to the ongoing video conference call that began on Thursday morning. For us, the rest of the world has faded away. We have somehow stumbled into this tunnel that is just us and the war, the war and us. I strain to catch familiar voices, even if I can only make out single words from the kitchen table. The absence of agitation indicates a momentary lull in activity.

My partner fills me in on the news of the day. The European Union has reached an agreement to impose sanctions on Putin and Lavrov, while Russia has vetoed a UN Security Council resolution demanding its withdrawal from Ukraine. The international community grapples with finding an appropriate response to Putin's action. One that will send a strong message, but will not send us straight to World War III.

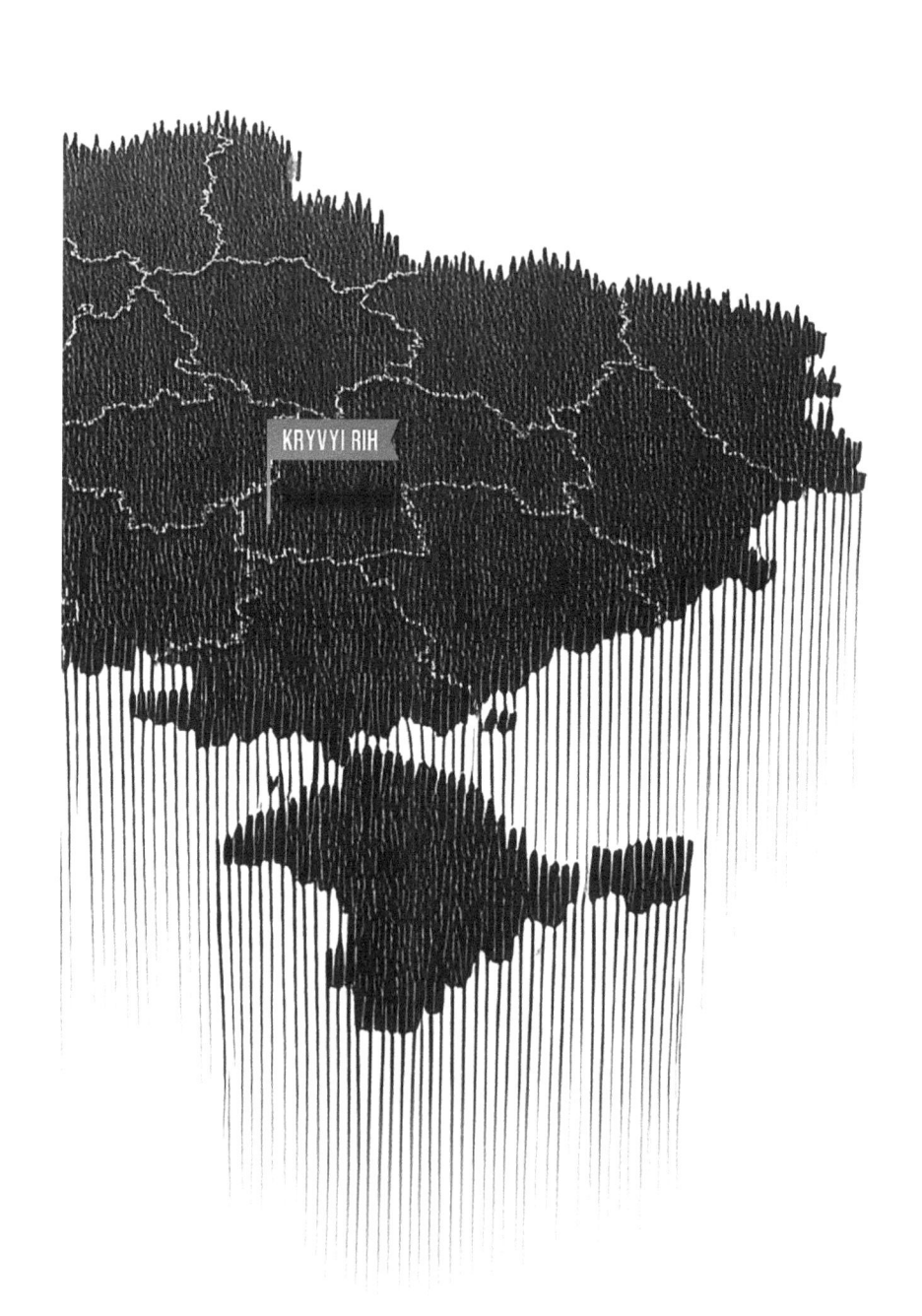

KRYVYI RIH

Chapter 5

Stay or run?

25 February 2022

Around 8pm there is some movement. Olena receives multiple messages from families who find themselves stranded at the Shehyni border crossing. Among those reaching out for help is Vitalii, one of our DevOps engineers. He is a devoted father to three children—two girls and a boy. The family is based in Kryvyi Rih, a city of 600,000 located in midwestern Ukraine. Until yesterday, life in the city's suburbs had been tranquil.

In their household, Vitalii's son Andriy was typically the first to rise each morning, and would announce the new day with an enthusiastic bounce onto his parents' bed. Age three and brimming with energy, he was eagerly looking forward to reuniting with his friends at daycare. Vitalii's daughters Anastasia and Natalyia were quieter in nature. Neither of them an early bird, they required a little more coaxing to leave their beds each morning. Sharing a room in their two-storey house, the sisters had their own unique dynamics. Vitalii cherished the mornings spent with his family. While his wife Diana prepared bowls of oatmeal with honey, he took care of the children, indulging in moments of togetherness before the day's activities commenced. Anastasia, at the age of six, and Natalyia, who had just turned eight, were growing into independent young girls. They could brush their teeth and comb their long blond hair mostly by themselves, with supervision and gentle nudges on days when sleepiness lingered a little longer.

This Thursday had started so differently. By the time Andriy rose, Vitalii was already wide awake. He had received multiple messages from friends who lived closer to the Russian border. Andriy found his father sitting at the kitchen table, his head resting in one of his hands, the index finger of the other hand scrolling through news reports and videos on his iPhone. Andriy rubbed his sleepy eyes as he approached his father, sensing the tension in the room. He climbed onto the chair next to Vitalii and peered at the screen, trying to understand what captured his father's attention. Vitalii looked up from his phone and mustered a smile showing his close-set pearly whites as he noticed Andriy's curious look. He shifted his gaze towards the door, where Diana was leaning against the doorway. Her weight rested on one leg, the other crossed over, matching her folded arms. She wore her hair in the usual loose bun and Vitalii could see the worry etched on her face. 'What shall we do?' she asked, and gently stroked Andriy's hair, as he had snuggled up to her in the meantime, clinging to her leg with his small fingers. 'I don't know,' Vitalii replied. 'For now, let's keep the children at home and monitor the news. I will reach out to our friends for more information on the situation further east. We will find a way to keep our family safe.'

His friends in Kharkiv, Donetsk, and Mariupol were all weighing their options. Some had already packed their bags, remaining vigilant and ready to evacuate at a moment's notice. Others had opted to leave their cities and seek refuge with family members in safer regions such as Lviv. Yet others felt a deep sense of duty and were contemplating taking up arms to defend their country.

In the meantime, his Telegram app was flooding with horrifying images. Destroyed houses, abandoned corpses, lost children. Diana's words echoed the fear in his heart. 'This is our glimpse into the future, Vitalii,' she said. 'This could be us tomorrow.' He found himself at a crossroads, grappling with the turmoil and uncertainty around him. Due to his heavy asthma, he had been exempted from military service when he was fourteen. However, his friends were right that he had a responsibility to fight for his country.

Running away from the situation felt morally conflicting, while staying felt irresponsible. His decision would have implications not only for his own safety but also for the future of his children.

Diana and Vitalii spent the afternoon packing their bags while the children watched a Disney film. Then, over dinner, they made a snap decision.

As the clock struck midnight, they got into the car. The Toyota was packed to the brim. The children, unaware of the gravity of the situation, slept soundly in the backseat, covered up to their necks with a warm blanket. Vitalii adjusted his rearview mirror, struggling to catch sight of the road behind them. The boot was stacked with suitcases, every inch of the back row filled with bags of clothes and personal belongings.

As they set out into the night, the familiar streets of Kryvyi Rih gradually faded from view. They stayed on the main road past the city of Uman and towards Lviv and the border crossing to Poland at Shehyni. The journey that stretched before them like a lifeline was a thousand-kilometre drive across the country. News of air raids in Zaporizhzhya reached them, a city that was a mere 160 kilometres from their home in Kryvyi Rih. Russian troops steadily approached the city's nuclear power plant while local civilian defence forces dug trenches to defend critical bridge positions and prepare for what seemed like an imminent confrontation. The proximity left them with a chilling realisation of the peril that awaited those who had not fled in time. As the kilometres passed beneath the wheels of the car, Vitalii's grip on the steering wheel tightened.

Seven hours into their journey, they were approaching the city of Vinnytsia with their fuel gauge worryingly close to empty. The news on the radio and Telegram reported hour-long queues snaking out from gas stations across the country. With thousands on the move, they could not cope with the demand. Diana's fingers danced over her phone screen as she frantically searched for the shortest queues. They succumbed to necessity half an hour later, joining the tail of a queue that sprawled out along the main road leading out of the city. The line was so extensive that its end dissolved into the horizon. For more than two tortuous hours, the car inched forward in a sluggish progression, while Google Maps recalibrated their ETA with maddening regularity, each update pushing their anticipated arrival at the border deeper into the afternoon.

When they finally reached the perimeter of the gas station, Vitalii quickly replenished the car's tank and snagged two coffees and a stash of energy drinks at the checkout. With at least six more hours to go, he would need them.

When the family finally reached Shehyni, more than fifteen weary hours from the comfort of their home, they were hungry and exhausted. But they queued again. They had been inching steadily towards the checkpoint metre by metre for the past five hours. Upon checking Google Maps, Vitalii was disheartened to realise that they were still more than five kilometres away from the actual checkpoint. The minutes turned into hours, and their patience began wearing thin.

--

Around 8pm, Vitalii messages Olena to ask for help. We jump into action, relieved to be needed and able to do something purposeful. I book a hotel room for the family through Expedia and send Vitalii the instructions for check-in, hoping that they will soon get a rest in a comfortable hotel room. However, when they arrive twenty minutes later, the young receptionist apologetically informs them that the hotel is fully booked and is not cooperating with Expedia. Confusion and frustration hang in the air, as I question how I was able to make an online booking through the platform. There goes my feeling of being of service. Trying not to be discouraged, I scour booking.com and find another hotel. This time, luck is on our side, and the family finally falls into bed, planning to get back in line at the border crossing the next morning.

Chapter 6

Wrestling with the grind

26 February 2022

It is the early hours of Saturday. Staying up to date on the situation in Ukraine is difficult. No city can be considered safe, with the constant threat of attacks looming over the entire country at all times. While the timing and frequency of the bombings are unpredictable, terror at dawn remains the only constant. Breaks in between shelling are for counting the dead, checking on your home and belongings, and moving from one shelter to another if you really have to do so. There is visible destruction, and images of rubble and ashes circulating the globe. And there is the equally active but invisible threat that receives less media attention: cyber attacks. These assaults paralyse critical systems that uphold order in daily life, govern states, and maintain essential infrastructure for communities.

As official communication and internet access become increasingly unstable in Ukraine, people are turning to social media to organise themselves. Considered less vulnerable to cyber attacks and popular among the Ukrainian population, Telegram has become the messaging app of choice for many. In response to the crisis, hundreds of channels have been created on the platform overnight. They serve various purposes, such as tracking the situation in specific neighbourhoods, organising defence groups, facilitating donations, and sharing information about evacuation modes and routes. The abundance of channels is overwhelming, but we do not want to miss any crucial information, so we subscribe to most channels we come across. We create one for our employees as well that we name after our company.

Making sense of the flood of information is challenging. It is day three of my learning Ukrainian. My language skills lag way behind my tasks. In desperate need of a hack, I discover the camera function on my Google Translate app. Hovering my phone over the Ukrainian text in the Telegram groups on my laptop screen allows the app to translate the text into English instantly. This is how I will spend most of my days from now on.

Our goal for today is to get organised. With more than eighty employees and their loved ones in Ukraine to support, and only four of us on the call outside of the country, it is easy to lose track, and we cannot afford even the smallest mistake. Overnight, we feel that we have become essential care workers with responsibilities that require the utmost accuracy.

To streamline our efforts, we create a list on Notion, Danylo's favourite online workspace for notes that we typically use for our projects. It includes the names of all employees and their family members, along with details such as pets, passport numbers, mode of transport, current locations, next stops, and final destinations. We colour-code it, too: green for recently contacted individuals, amber for open requests or those requiring a follow-up, and red for urgent needs.

Due to the language barrier, Danylo and Olena take on the task of calling each team member, while Larissa and I primarily rely on messaging to provide support. Many of the names on the list are unfamiliar to us, as there has been limited interaction between our team and the developers in the past. We work for the same company, but focus on separate projects with little overlap. We aim to stay in contact with our team daily, carefully tracking their movements and well-being, and decide to assign a contact person for each employee. We hope this will allow us to distribute the workload and address individual needs swiftly, following the principle of 'divide and conquer' that we often employ in project management.

I cannot help but notice how much of our everyday language is tied to war-related metaphors that now feel terribly misplaced. We used to say that we 'create a war room, call the shots, choose our battles, and dodge a bullet.'

Around noon, I start typing a message to Theo. Crafting it takes me more than thirty minutes. I repeatedly type and delete. I struggle to find words that are considerate but not inquisitive, understanding but not disrespectful, not too calm or too dramatic. Six hours pass, and still, there is no reply. I cannot help but worry and wonder if others in our group are experiencing the same feelings. Feeling anxious, I whisper softly, 'Hello?', on the call. Within seconds, Danylo, Larissa, and Olena turn on their video and unmute themselves. We have become a reliable support system, with one of us always there to respond. All day, all night. As we exchange status updates, it becomes evident that we have to change our strategy. Danylo and Olena have barely managed to call twenty people from their list.

The need for people to be heard, to share their experiences, and to grapple with the overwhelming changes of the past three days is so pressing that every call takes much longer than we had accounted for in our planning. Their first conversations feel unstructured and tumultuous. They do not know how to engage with people in Kharkiv and other places facing severe attacks. Olena empathises with their pain but feels overwhelmed by their grief as well as her own. It is a draining task. How could we expect someone who is experiencing the pain firsthand to provide trauma relief to others?

Absent a better idea, we persevere, using Telegram messaging as an alternative to phone calls when they need distance to cope. Each case and conversation is markedly different. Some colleagues are nervous and emotional, struck by shock and uncertain about their next steps. Others remain quiet and composed. They comprehend the situation and have a clear plan.

After several calls, Olena begins to find her voice. The initial feeling of being overwhelmed has subsided, and connecting with them makes her feel like she can make a difference. It offers respite from the terrifying thoughts that are constantly swirling in her mind. The glimpses of hope keep us going, solidarity grounds us, and connection fuels us. There is the news of local volunteers reclaiming territory from the Russian forces, a family who managed to escape a city under attack unharmed, and gratitude for our companionship of employees who are stuck in bomb shelters.

Nevertheless, it is an excruciating task that leaves me feeling drained. For Danylo and Olena, I try to remain rational, helpful, and supportive. I want to be someone steady on whom they can lean. Fifty-five hours into our Google Meet conference, this is becoming challenging. The exhaustion from lack of sleep, the permanent flood of terrifying news on all channels, and the persistent worry for every single person on our list have turned me into an emotional wreck. It is a particular kind of guilt that accompanies these feelings. After all, this is not my war. It is not my country under attack, nor my countrymen enduring torment. My pain feels illegitimate. I have no right to fall apart. My role is to be strong for this team.

Chapter 7

And then he laughs

26 February 2022

Around 5.30pm, I excuse myself for half an hour. I change into sweatpants, slip on my running shoes, grab my gloves and head out the door. I dash down the four storeys to the main entry of our building, taking two stairs at a time, my left hand gliding along the handrail and propelling me around each landing. Escaping the confines of my living room, I feel a surge of energy course through me. I open the front door and am greeted by a gust of cold air as the temperature hovers around seven degrees Celsius. I turn left and make my way towards Monbijou Park, situated alongside the calm river Spree. The park is a popular spot for dog owners, and today is no exception. A man wrapped in a thick blue shawl throws a Frisbee and smiles as he watches his Labrador pace off to retrieve it. Nearby, a young couple plays with their adorable Cavoodle puppy. They are my reminder that amidst the chaos, normal life still exists.

I continue my run, crossing the short bridge to Museum Island and turning left towards one of Berlin's most renowned roads, 'Unter den Linden'. The sleet-covered path will lead me towards the iconic Brandenburg Gate. I feel my eyes glisten with tears that flow uncontrollably down my cheeks by now. The moisture, mixed with the cold, adds a chill to my already flushed skin. I lengthen my stride, almost leaping from one foot to the other. With each metre covered, I feel a sense of relief. I find solace in running till the pain in my legs numbs my heart. I sprint till my body is too exerted to focus on anything other than the task at hand: placing one foot in front of the other and navigating the slippery cobblestones that pave Berlin's streets. Passing through the grand Brandenburg Gate, I turn towards the Reichstag and head back towards home. Now that I have somewhat cleared my head, I am eager to get back on the call.

The number of people seeking to cross the border grows, and our search for temporary accommodation becomes yet more challenging. The border crossings have transformed into arduous multi-day waiting games:

Yagodin border crossing: 3,900 cars in line, twenty-four hours' wait
Ustyluh border crossing: 1,800 cars in line, sixty-two hours' wait
Shehyni border crossing: 2,550 cars in line, thirty-eight hours' wait

Traditional housing options are becoming scarce as an influx of people moves from east to west, seeking refuge from Russia's destruction and towards the safety of European borders. Hotels, holiday homes, bed & breakfasts, guest houses, hostels, farm stays, and cottages quickly get booked. Those who can do so generously open their homes to tired strangers in need of a rest on their way out of the country. Within minutes, private rooms find occupants through Telegram and Facebook groups.

It is getting late and several families are still on the move when one of them reaches a breaking point. Exhausted and famished after a strenuous journey across the country, they are in desperate need of a place to rest near Vinnytsia, a small city located southwest of Kyiv. They message our company's group on Telegram, asking for help.

Despite our best efforts, our search for accommodation yields no results. I keep refreshing Google, Expedia, Booking.com, and Tripadvisor. Every booking platform comes up empty; there does not seem to be a single free bed within a hundred-kilometre radius of Vinnytsia. In a race against time,

Larissa and I keep searching for smaller places on Google Maps that may not be listed on traditional booking platforms while Danylo calls them one by one.

Hope hangs by a thread, and Danylo is tense. He has barely had any sleep since Thursday, and his eyes are bloodshot and his face pale and puffy. The worry and responsibility are taking their toll on him, too, and the typical twinkle in his eyes has long vanished. Although he is muted while he is on the phone, his body language speaks volumes. I can see him nervously fidget with his hands and fiddle with the seam of his blue T-shirt. He gives us a disappointed look, shaking his head. No luck yet. The search goes on.

A glimmer of hope appears as a notification lights up my phone screen. It is a message from Vadym, one of our lead back-end developers, in our company's Telegram channel. He mentions an intriguing accommodation near Vinnytsia—apparently, there is a 'man full of food and a bunch of cool honey'. That is what Google Translate tells me. I imagine a farm owned by a corpulent beekeeper, known for his bountiful harvests. Whatever it is exactly, it sounds like a solution to our problem. The excitement on my face is catching Danylo's attention. 'Any news, Stef?' he asks.

'Yes! Vadym found accommodation,' I blurt out excitedly. 'It is a man full of food with a bunch of cool honey. A beekeeper's farm, I assume. Check out his message on Telegram.'

Danylo unlocks his phone. As he reads the message, he hesitates for a second before bursting into uncontrollable laughter, the kind that shakes your entire body and leaves you breathless. How I missed this sound! He folds his arms on his desk, rests his head on them, and keeps chuckling. I do not quite understand what is going on, but hear myself joining in. It feels liberating. The weight of our overwhelming circumstances momentarily falls off our shoulders. For a brief moment, time stands still. The clock has turned back to 23 February, when we were just a close-knit group of colleagues working together, building new products, and finding joy in the process.

After regaining his composure, he says, 'There is no beekeeper, Stef. I have no idea how Google Translate came up with that, but Vadym has indeed found accommodation for the night.'

With tonight's problem solved, we shift our focus to the weeks ahead. Just like the day before, I have lost all sense of space and time. My partner enters the living room and leaves a plate of my favourite meal, a homemade Indian spinach curry, on my desk. I chew it listlessly, my mind consumed by the relentless research. I push myself to avoid breaks. They give way to contemplation, worry, and mental images that scare me.

In our modest one-bedroom apartment, I leave the door to the living room open at all times. While I shamble to the kitchen to get a cup of tea, I seek comfort in the familiar voices emanating from my laptop's speakers. Leaving the call is out of the question, as I do not want to miss anything. An opportunity to help. To take action. To do something in a situation where most of the world is condemned to watch helplessly from the sidelines.

Later that night, the beep of our phones announces another message in our company's Telegram channel. Mykhailo Fedorov, Ukraine's Minister of Digital Transformation, has announced the formation of an IT Army, and is seeking volunteers with coding or hacking skills. The new army is envisioned to serve a dual purpose. An offensive cyber unit will conduct digital espionage operations against invading Russian forces and target military entities, while a defensive unit will protect critical infrastructure within Ukraine. Like most other efforts, the IT Army will rely on social media platforms such as Twitter and Telegram to organise itself and coordinate the efforts of volunteers.

Four of our employees have already signed up for it and are calling for others to join them. 'This war will last,' France's president, Emanuel Macron, said today, and millions of Ukrainians are bracing for it. Like Vitalii's friends in Kharkiv, some of our employees feel compelled to take more direct action, and are preparing to take up arms. Among them is Farid, a German colleague who relocated to Ukraine only six months ago.

LVIV

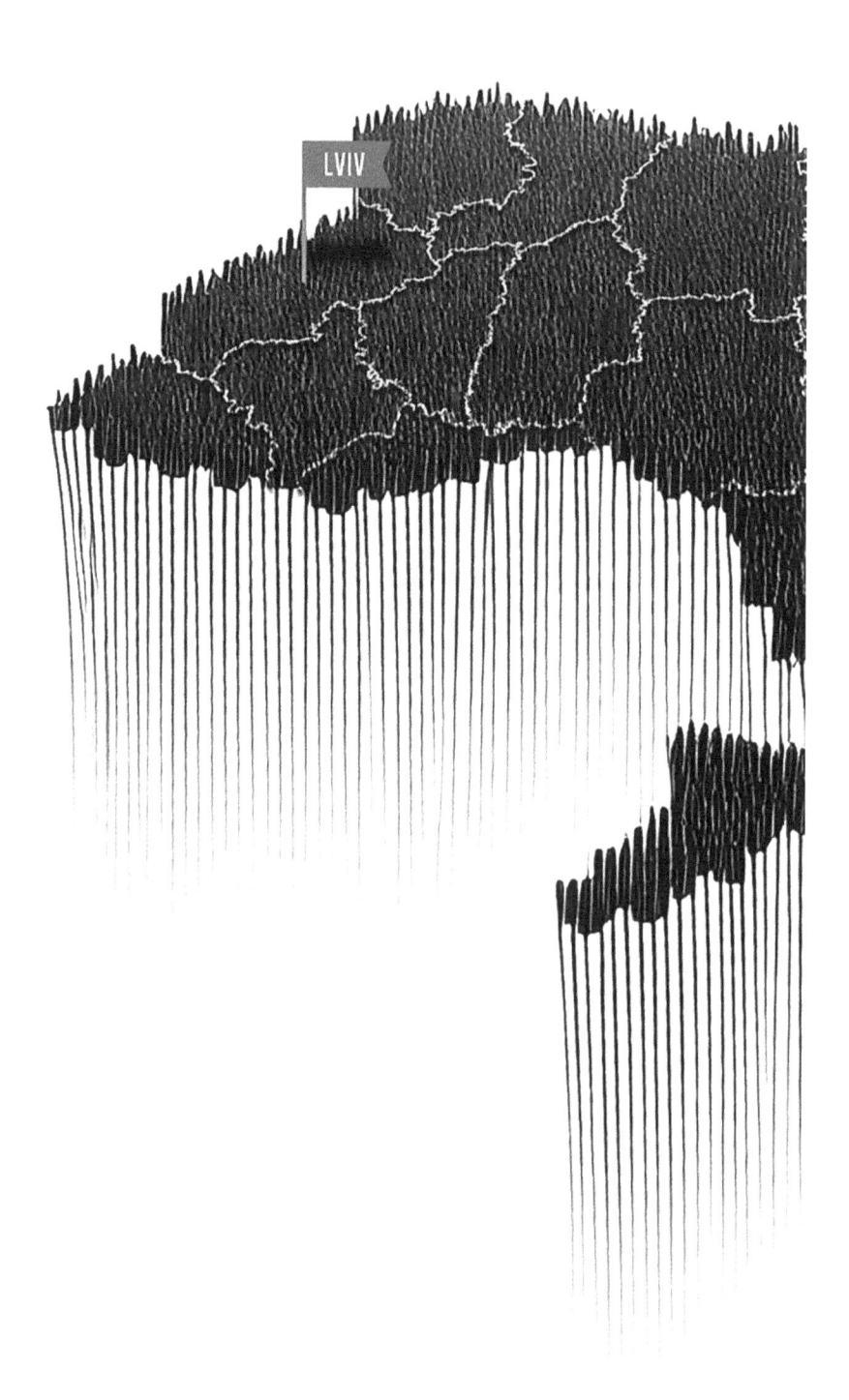

Chapter 8

Vodka, love, and sacrifice

27 February 2022

I wake up at 5.30am, half an hour before the alarm I set the previous night. I am reluctant to grab my phone from the night table next to my bed, dreading the distressing news notifications that might have appeared during the early hours of the day. I try to doze off again but my mind remains wide awake. After fifteen minutes of futile efforts, I surrender to the elusiveness and trudge to the bathroom to invigorate myself with a splash of cold water on my face. Back in the kitchen, I brew a fresh cup of coffee that I hope will provide me with a jolt of energy.

By 6am, I am once again back on our call. Our daily rhythm feels like a lifelong routine by now. Olena has assumed the helm from Danylo at 5am and is already online. With many of our employees traversing Ukraine by train, bus, and car, our Telegram group is tranquil for the moment. We seize this respite to catch up on the latest news and engage in discussions about our most cherished family recipes—a seemingly mundane subject, but one that provides us with a much-needed sense of normality. We treasure each passing second of it. The events of the past four days have taught us that it will not last long.

Overnight, Russian troops have been steadily pushing towards Kyiv, Kharkiv, and Kherson in Ukraine's eastern regions. However, their advances have been met with resolute resistance. According to the local news, Ukrainian defence forces have successfully destroyed over 150 tanks, twenty-six helicopters, and seven fighter jets. Hundreds of Russian soldiers have lost their lives or been captured as prisoners of war. Reading the reports, I find myself pondering a sombre question: How many of these soldiers were truly aware of the purpose they were sent to fulfil, and how many among them genuinely supported such actions? If they did not, what is their moral duty of questioning or refusing orders?

Shortly after 8am, Larissa joins the call, followed by our CEO.

'Farid reached out to me this morning,' he announces. 'He crossed the border to Poland on Thursday but will be returning to Lviv soon. He can transport goods for us. Let's prepare a list of items we need to transform our office into a shelter and support the team members who have volunteered for the army.'

Larissa and I exchange a perplexed look. Are we about to deliver weapons? Is this what this war has turned us into—arms dealers?

'Stef, Larissa, can you compile a list of things Farid can take?' the CEO asks. I find myself nodding, unsure of what exactly I am agreeing to. Ironically, he is assigning this task to the two pacifists within our company. We possess no knowledge of warfare, weaponry, defensive gear, or protection. Shortly after, he and Olena leave the call to attend to their young children. While our world has ground to a halt since Thursday, their toddlers' needs have remained unchanged. For them, it is just another Sunday, though they may sense that something is amiss.

I wonder what thoughts must be swirling through Farid's mind right now. A German in his mid-thirties, he was one of the very first employees to join the company. With his outgoing nature and infectious buoyancy, he connects with people effortlessly, drawing them in with sincere interest and curiosity. This remarkable trait led to his recruiting me for the team. In the tumultuous days of March 2020, as the world was grappling with the onset of the Covid-19 pandemic, Farid embarked on his own entrepreneurial journey. Having closely observed innovation practices within various companies for several years, he recognised the need for a software solution that could assist organisations in collecting, organising, and evaluating new ideas. In December 2020, he approached me on LinkedIn with an invitation for a virtual introductory coffee, seeking my feedback on his idea. I agreed without hesitation, and what followed was a stimulating conversation that lasted well over an hour. I was captivated by his clever questioning, which effortlessly turned light-hearted conversations into profound discussions, and touched by his genuine kindness. After our call, Farid suggested connecting me with the CEO and founder of another company. A few months later, in March 2021, I became part of this company, all thanks to Farid's initiative.

He regularly engaged with our Ukrainian colleagues and felt increasingly drawn to the country. In September 2021, he relocated to Lviv for three months. The local team eagerly welcomed him, and introduced him to the city, the office, and Ukraine's impressive variety of exquisite spirits similar to vodka, the so-called *horilka*. Following Ukrainian custom, which involves raising a glass to the good, the bad, the unexpected, and the long-awaited moments, the group spent most evenings together. He learned to distinguish Nemiroff vodka from Khortytsa *horilka*, and to understand the silver filtration technologies needed to create the proper Khor Platinum spirit. He developed a keen palate, proud to be able to identify the spicy rye aroma in Zirkova One.

However, deciphering the thoughts and feelings of the Ukrainians whom he encountered proved to be a challenge. Their emotions were rarely readily displayed on their faces. For weeks, Farid found it difficult to discern whether they regarded him as a friend or a mere acquaintance. They were hardworking, honest, and true to their word. While they did not engage in much conversation during the day, a few glasses of *horilka* in the evening would loosen them up, revealing their wonderful sense of humour.

As the days went by, Farid's affection for Ukraine grew. By the time he was planning to return home in December, he had fallen in love with the country and decided to stay. He secured an apartment just a short stroll away from the office, relishing the opportunity to walk down Petra Doroshenka Street each morning, where lush green cherry trees lined the way.

Turning left into Stefanyka Street before reaching the city centre, he would pass through Ivan-Franko Park, a public garden popular among dog owners. He crossed paths with the same bearded man walking his French bulldog each morning and exchanged a brief nod of acknowledgement. Bohdana Lepkoho Street would take him north, crossing a bustling intersection, before he would continue towards Lviv's State University of Internal Affairs, a magnificent white brick building adorned with a small circular window. Most days, Farid would take a small detour to visit a coffee shop named 'Tsikava' for his first shot of espresso and a delectable custard pastry topped with blueberries. He was settling in well.

In the early morning hours of 24 February, he woke from a groggy slumber, his head heavy from the last glass of *horilka* he had reluctantly indulged in the night before. It took him a few moments to comprehend the distant sound seeping into his consciousness. The robust windows of his apartment, designed to withstand the harsh Ukrainian winters, effectively blocked external noise as well as they did cold. Irritated, he rolled over in his bed and pulled the quilt over his head, attempting to muffle the unwelcome disturbance and drift back to sleep.

However, as the sound grew more distinct, a sudden realisation jolted him awake—this was the sound of an air raid siren. Hastily, he retrieved his phone from the charger on his bedside table and unlocked it to check his notifications. At the top of the list was a message from his best friend in Germany, saying 'Farid, get out of here immediately.' Sitting upright in bed, he scanned the news. His Ukrainian still was not good enough to read the local news without the assistance of Google Translate, but he could grasp single words. It was enough for him to discern that Chernihiv and Kharkiv had been targeted by Russian military forces this morning. As he had anticipated, the invasion focused on the eastern regions. 'The air raid sirens here in Lviv must be merely precautionary measures,' he murmured to himself. With a flicker of reassurance, he dialled the number of his friend Victor, who lived just a few blocks away and answered the call right away.

'Farid! It's happening, it's happening. Get ready, the Russians are coming. Find a bunker, head to the mountains, or leave for Poland as soon as you can. I'll fight and need to prepare now,' Victor's voice crackled with urgency.

Farid barely had a chance to utter a word in response before Victor hung up on him. He sounded seriously concerned but had a tendency for excitement and thrilling tales which left Farid seeking a second opinion. He swiftly called his colleague Iurii, a local Ukrainian in his mid-forties known for his composed nature and rare display of nerves. Unfortunately, Iurii's perspective offered little solace.

'I'm not sure if I should stay or run. I want to help, but I'm scared. Will they really attack Lviv? What would you do, Iurii?' Farid inquired.

'Lviv is not safe, Farid. You have two options, and you need to act immediately. You can either seek shelter in the mountains outside Lviv or make your way to Poland. If I were in your position, I'd choose the latter,' Iurii responded calmly but resolutely.

As he ended the call, Farid's hands trembled uncontrollably. Visions of rockets raining down from the sky upon the city flooded his consciousness. Seeking composure, he opened the window and allowed fresh air to fill his lungs as he took a deep breath. Outside, the air was thick with unease. Agitated voices echoed through the streets as throngs of people hurried past, too many for this time of day. Parents clasped their children's hands tightly as they urged them to hasten their steps. The trams passing by his apartment building were crammed to capacity.

His apartment was located between the central station and Lviv's military base. Checking his intended route to Poland on Google Maps, he would have to follow the road along the train tracks for three kilometres to leave the city. It was a perilous undertaking, considering that railway infrastructure served as a prime target for disrupting supply lines and troop movements. If he passed through at the wrong time, his car could be caught in the shelling.

Seized by a sudden surge of adrenaline, Farid lunged for the duffel bag he had stashed under the bed just the day before. He tossed handfuls of his most prized possessions into his backpack, his hands trembling with the realisation that had it not been for Victor's prescient warning, he would now be in a much more precarious situation. Less than twenty-four hours earlier, his car was nothing more than a lifeless shell, its tank empty, its battery dead. He had wilfully ignored the murmurs of caution that had suggested he prepare for the possibility of an attack, and neglected to secure cash, hoard provisions, and pack a bag with essential supplies. When Victor offered to jump-start his vehicle, Farid had initially waved him off nonchalantly. Fortunately, his friend had insisted, and vehemently urged him to take precautions when he noticed Farid's lack of preparation. Since he needed to charge the battery by driving anyway, Farid had decided to fill the tank and procure some cash and emergency provisions yesterday. Now, as he bolted from the room, he felt grateful to Victor, his fingers clenched around the keys that were his ticket to salvation.

As he stepped through his front door, he found himself thrust into chaos. A line of people stretched across the street, spanning at least a hundred metres, eagerly awaiting their turn at the ATM. Taxis passed by with their lights off, transporting only close friends and family members at this critical time. His phone buzzed incessantly with calls and messages from concerned friends abroad, checking on his well-being. However, he was well aware that data and battery life would soon become scarce resources. If this truly was a nationwide invasion, it was only a matter of time before the first rockets would descend upon Lviv. Once he crossed the border into Poland, he would have ample time to respond to them.

Rejecting the incoming calls from abroad, he dialled the numbers of his friends residing in Lviv instead. As he shut the car door and embarked on the drive towards the outskirts of the city, he checked in on each of them sequentially, and offered to pick them up on his way to the border. However, not a single one accepted. They had all decided to stay. Just as Iurii and Victor had told him earlier, three of them were preparing to join Ukraine's armed forces right away, too.

Talking to them, he could not help but feel an overwhelming sense of respect for their courage. His friend Daria had just reentered the workforce as an IT recruiter after dedicating the past five years to caring for her children. The chivalry and protectiveness she typically expected from the men around her had once made him consider her a 'princess'—charming and elegant, yet fragile when it came to serious matters. Today, her determination was resolute. Within a few weeks, she would hold a weapon in her hands for the very first time in her life.

Farid had already reached the highway beyond the train tracks when his phone buzzed with an incoming call from Mati. His friend was planning to remain in Lviv but now found himself in the company of an American friend who required urgent evacuation, fearing she would become a primary target for Russian forces or separatist groups. Farid was torn. He wanted to help, but Mati lived on the opposite side of the city. Returning to his location meant passing the train tracks once more and crossing the city centre, where he could get stuck in traffic for hours. After a fleeting moment of indecision, Farid stepped on the brakes and took a U-turn. The blaring sirens continued to echo throughout the city, rattling him to his core. When he finally reached Mati's apartment block, his fingers had turned pale from his tight grip on the steering wheel.

Mati stood outside, accompanied by a tall woman with long brown hair neatly tied up in a ponytail, whom Farid presumed to be Mati's American colleague. Their faces expressed a mixture of anxiety and relief as they caught sight of Farid's arrival. He turned on the hazard lights as he carefully brought the car to a halt on the side of the road, swiftly pressing the button to open the trunk. After briefly introducing himself, Farid helped Lisa, his newfound passenger, load her suitcase into the car. She was a graphic designer and a passionate painter who had been attracted by Lviv's vibrant cultural scene. A year prior, she had left her hometown of Seattle to settle in Lviv and work remotely for an American firm. She often frequented co-working spaces in the city centre, where she had crossed paths with Mati a few months earlier.

As Lisa settled into the passenger seat, Farid approached Mati to bid his friend a heartfelt farewell. He briefly contemplated persuading Mati to leave with him but recognised that it was not his place to challenge his friend's decision. Locking eyes for a moment, they exchanged a silent understanding. With a resolute nod of support, Farid turned away and got into the car.

The seventy-eight-kilometre drive to the border crossing in Korczowa-Krakowiec lasted two hours but seemed to stretch on for an eternity. During the journey, an eerie silence hung between them. Farid and Lisa focused on finding the optimal routes to avoid traffic and held their breaths as they repeated the journey along the train tracks from which Farid had returned not long ago. All of a sudden, Lisa broke the silence.

'Thank you for taking me,' she said. 'I didn't have time to think. When I realised what was happening I left everything behind and rushed to Mati's place. I didn't know what else to do.'

Finally, like the brothers Serhiy and Vlad, they managed to pass the border crossing, and were met by welcoming Polish volunteers on the other side. A profound wave of relief washed over Farid—he was safe.

Two hours later, he turned the doorknob to his room in the first bed and breakfast he stumbled upon near the highway exit in Rzeszów. Weary, he let his bags drop to the floor and collapsed onto the bed. Taking a moment to catch his breath, he inhaled deeply. His fingertips traced the delicate stitching of the brown cotton bedcover beneath him. He became aware of his heavy legs and the discomfort of his swollen feet confined within his shoes. Gradually, the events of the past hours began to seep into his consciousness. The faces of shock and disbelief of fellow travellers in the cars flooding across the border into Poland. Families, couples, and individuals alike, people from all walks of life, had found themselves catapulted abruptly into the same spot by the onslaught of Russia's attack.

The following day, Farid woke up with a foggy recollection of how he had drifted off to sleep. The night had been plagued by restlessness, with periods of staring at the ceiling, his veins still pulsating with the remnants of adrenaline from the previous day. He realised it was Friday, a typical workday for the German startup that employed him.

However, his mind felt clouded and disoriented, consumed by worrisome thoughts about his friends who remained in Lviv—those who were left behind, or much worse, were about to undergo training for the impending frontline. Recognising the need to restore his energy and recover from the past day, Farid decided to request a few days off from work.

He spent his first day in Rzeszów immersing himself in the news, diligently catching up on the latest developments. He reached out to family and friends, ensuring them that he was safe and unharmed before he wandered aimlessly through the streets of the town, engaging in conversations with the people he encountered along the way. Most of them shared his shock and concern, their minds grappling with the uncertainty of what the coming weeks might bring. He stayed in touch with his friends in Lviv through Telegram, a messaging app. The updates from the city appeared relatively calm, except those about the attacks on several military bases outside of Lviv that had occurred on Thursday morning.

He felt a tumultuous mix of fear, worry, anger, and guilt. He could not help but berate himself, feeling that he should have done more, cared more, and demonstrated courage instead of fleeing like a coward.

By Sunday morning, he had decided to return to Lviv and defend the country he had grown to love so deeply in recent months. He picked up his phone and dialled our CEO's number.

Farid in the Carpathian mountains, 2021

Chapter 9

We are all Ukrainians

27 February 2022

In Germany, Larissa and I start to compile a comprehensive list of essential items for Farid to transport across the border from Poland or source in Lviv with the help of the local team. We begin with the most straightforward necessities, focusing on things that will be crucial to transform the office into a temporary shelter for families who may arrive in Lviv from other parts of Ukraine. Air mattresses, bedsheets, and hygiene products are among our initial priorities. We include non-perishable groceries such as canned beans, meat, rice, condensed milk, and water. In consideration of the children, we include cookies, crackers, and chocolate—snacks with long shelf lives. We add shirts, pants, socks, and pullovers for warmth and protection against the harsh temperatures of Lviv's February, and batteries and chargers compatible with most common models of phones and laptops. Equally crucial are first aid kits, meticulously assembled with pain relievers, antibiotics, antiseptics, and bandages to address any immediate medical needs.

As we progress, our focus shifts towards researching the necessary medical equipment to treat war-related injuries effectively. I find myself seated on the floor of our living room, swathed in a comforting blanket and deeply absorbed in the wealth of information displayed on my laptop screen.

It is a Sunday unlike any other in our lives. Hours pass unnoticed as we immerse ourselves in the intricacies of military weaponry and medical supplies. I learn about tanks, grenades, and mines, and to distinguish between submachine guns, shotguns, and machine guns. I grasp the specialised medical resources needed to attend to a glancing shot versus a direct hit, the range of a sniper rifle, and the odds of survival contingent on the angle of impact. I learn of the injuries that military protective gear can avert, and the irreversible loss of limb it cannot prevent.

I find myself increasingly wrestling with the ethics of arms delivery and my pacifist beliefs. Yet again, I come eye to eye with the privilege of having lived in a peaceful environment all my life. Proclaiming the virtues of peace comes easily when one's own home remains untouched by bombs, one's own family is safe from assault, and one's own country is not under the threat of invasion. Everyone deserves the right to defend themselves against injustice, and the means to do so. While the idea of supplying arms weighs on my conscience, depriving anyone of this fundamental right stirs an even greater disquiet within me.

The clock strikes noon, and my partner enters the room, the smell of lunch wafting through the air. Concerned for my well-being, he gently suggests, 'I think you should eat something and leave the house for a little while. The sun is shining, and a break from this might do you good.'

Glancing towards Larissa, I see her nodding in agreement. Our constant presence on the call has made us part of each other's household, most often as witnesses, but sometimes as active participants in day-to-day conversations.

'Sounds like a good idea, Stef. Let's send the list to Farid and get out for a bit,' Larissa agrees.

After a refreshing shower, I hop on my bike and make my way towards Berlin's iconic Brandenburg Gate. Since Thursday, citizens across Europe have called for demonstrations against Russia's invasion. Determined to lend my voice to the cause outside of our company, I decide to join Berlin's protest this afternoon. As I cross the Spree River, I witness a steady stream of people converging from all directions. I lock my bike securely a few streets away and merge with the crowd, following the throng towards 'Straße des 17. Juni', one of Berlin's most renowned streets spanning eighty-five metres and linking the Brandenburg Gate in the east with Ernst-Reuter-Platz in the west.

The mass of people has transformed into a vibrant sea of blue and yellow, adorned with flags, posters, and painted faces. Messages such as 'Stop the war', 'Europe stands with Ukraine,' and 'We are all Ukrainians' can be read on the banners held high. I march slowly and feel the goose bumps on my skin multiply with every step. Over 100,000 people have gathered here in a powerful display of protest. After almost four days on the call, engaged in the seemingly insurmountable battle against a superpower, it feels like we are not alone. People from all corners of Europe are taking to the streets and demanding action from their governments. Danylo shares a photo of the demonstration he is attending in Amsterdam. I promptly respond with a photo of the swelling crowd surrounding me in Berlin. Being 700 kilometres apart from each other, we are bound together by a shared spirit. My thoughts turn to our team, and I hope they feel the same sense of unity and support. I long for them to know that we stand with them.

Just after 6.30pm, long after I have returned home, a colleague in Ukraine responds with a photo capturing the golden hues of the sunset meeting the clear blue sky—nature painting Ukraine's national flag on the horizon.

Demonstration against Russia's invasion in Berlin, February 2022

Chapter 10

A new home

27 February 2022

We spend the early evening of Sunday eagerly tracking the location of our first bus on Google Maps, which departed from Krakow at 9am today. For the past three days, we have been urging the bus drivers to remain in Poland, hoping we would be able to fill all fifty-seven seats with our employees and their families, whom we are deeply committed to evacuating safely.

However, many of them remain hesitant to embark on this uncertain journey and prefer to stay in Ukraine, keeping a vigilant eye on the rapidly unfolding situation. It is a daunting proposition to leave one's cherished home and loved ones behind for the prospect of an unknown future, devoid of any guaranteed return date. It implies navigating a foreign language, foreign customs, foreign people, and foreign bureaucratic systems, all while relying on the kindness and goodwill of strangers. None of us willingly seek the status of a refugee as long as even the faintest glimmer of hope for a safer alternative persists.

The imposition of martial law has further complicated matters, prohibiting men aged eighteen through sixty years from leaving the country, with exemptions granted only in rare cases, thereby forcing families into painful separations. Others are enduring the harrowing reality of constant shelling by the Russian forces in their areas. For them, venturing beyond the safety of the bomb shelters is a treacherous gamble, followed by a long and hazardous journey across Ukraine in overcrowded trains or traffic jams.

By now, I know most of the Notion cards we use to keep track of our employees' well-being by heart. Lives that were new to me a mere four days ago have become intimately familiar. The names and stories of their protagonists have woven their way into the fabric of ours. Oleh and his expectant wife, Darya, in the bomb shelter. Ivan, Kateryna, and their two children on the westward journey from their home in Kyiv. Vitalii and his family, determined to make another attempt to leave Ukraine together.

Sadly, only a handful of seats on the bus today are occupied. Serhiy and his brother Vlad are sitting in the first two rows on the right side. Apart from the two drivers, they are the sole passengers in the vast vehicle. It is 8pm and they are a mere hour away from their final destination. The landscape outside has changed remarkably in the past twelve hours since their departure from Krakow. Their route led them northwest, traversing through Poland and passing the city of Wrocław before crossing the border into Germany. The autobahn to Berlin crossed through picturesque national parks and passed glistening reservoirs. They stopped for a brief break approximately fifty kilometres outside of Germany's capital, which allowed the drivers to swap their roles and adhere to the legal restrictions stipulating a maximum of eight consecutive hours behind the wheel for each of them. By the time they resume the westward journey toward their destination in Germany, the world outside is cloaked in darkness.

Meanwhile, in this quaint town, Larissa and our CEO diligently load the trunk of his car with the groceries they had bought the previous day. A palpable sense of anticipation hangs in the air, as neither of them knows what to expect. It felt like welcoming back a sibling who has been living abroad, with a complex cocktail of emotions. There is excitement and curiosity. For days, they have been looking forward to this moment, their anticipation fuelled by the messages exchanged with Serhiy. Larissa is eager to hear his tales, hoping his firsthand accounts will paint a more vivid picture of the situation on the ground. Beneath this excitement lingers anxiety and worry, with 'what ifs' echoing in her mind. What if Serhiy and Vlad find it hard to settle into their new environment? What if the city fails to meet their expectations? Most worryingly, what if recent events have scarred them, leaving them grappling with trauma?

Just after 9pm, the bus doors swing open. Serhiy and Vlad step out cautiously, their apprehension noticeable as they venture into the town that will become their home for the foreseeable future. Standing before them is our CEO, a somewhat reserved figure whom they remember from hiring interviews conducted over Zoom six months prior. Greetings are exchanged in halting English before they embark on the short drive to their temporary accommodation.

Always the meticulous planner, Larissa has managed to secure a holiday home for them until we can find them a more permanent residence. The three of them drop off their luggage and, to cap off the roller coaster of a day, decide to share a beer at the neighbouring pub. As their glasses clink together in a toast and smiles are exchanged, a wave of relief washes over our CEO. While the first bus's arrival did not yield the influx we had hoped for, one of our team members is safe. He feels a sense of protectiveness towards them take root, and makes a mental pledge to keep an eye on them and help them adjust to life in this new city to the best of his ability.

Just shy of midnight, Serhiy collapses into bed. The unfamiliar bed, though comfortable, fails to provide the solace of his treasured space back in Ukraine. His thoughts drift homeward. For a few seconds, he holds his breath and listens intently—deep inhales and exhales. Vlad seems to have found peaceful slumber already. Memories of their childhood rise unbidden. They had shared a room in the apartment they lived in back then, which was too cramped to house the entire family comfortably. In this quiet moment, Serhiy thinks of his mother, wondering if she too lies awake, her mind fraught with worry for her two sons to whom she did not have the chance to bid farewell properly. 'You've always said Vlad and I make the best team,' he muses internally. 'We'll get through this.'

CHOP

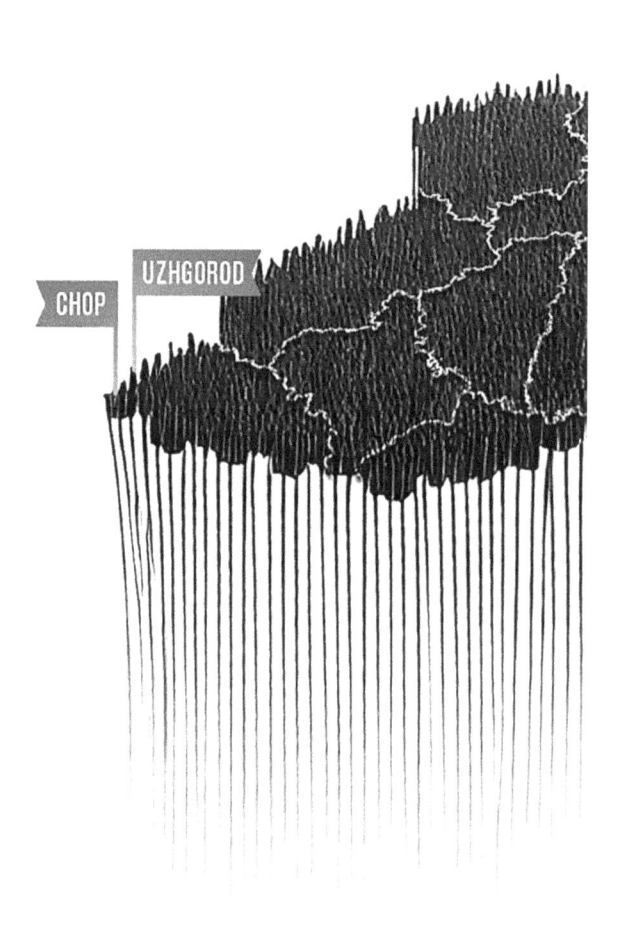

UZHGOROD

Chapter 11

Trapped

26–27 February 2022

After enduring more than fifteen hours in line, Vitalii and his family finally reach the border checkpoint in Uzhgorod. The clock strikes just past 11pm on Saturday. The officer collects their documents and bends down to take a look at the other passengers in the car through the driver's window. His gaze lands on the trio of children huddled together in the backseat, and he offers Diana a look of empathy. The weariness on their faces is evident.

Inside the car linger the scents of sliced meat, lemonade, and sleep deprivation. Children's books and games lie scattered across the backseat, and a teddy bear is squashed tightly against the side window. With their passports in hand, the border guard retreats to his booth. Vitalii exhales heavily and turns to Diana, his voice barely audible. 'It is going to be alright. We will be okay,' he whispers gently.

When the officer returns a few minutes later, he can tell things will not work out as smoothly as he had hoped.

'Your family is cleared to cross, but you have not been exempted from military service,' the officer announces in a stern tone. 'Martial law was declared on Friday, and you are required to remain in Ukraine until further notice, ready to be called to arms. Please decide now how you'd like to proceed. There are many people queued up behind you.'

Diana immediately interjects, her voice ringing with resolve, 'I won't go without you, Vitalii. Let's turn back.'

Vitalii takes a deep breath in, weighing his options in this agonising predicament. He could keep his family by his side, but how long would he be able to protect them in a war zone? Ushering them across the border into the European Union would provide them with a safer future. However, single-handedly caring for three children is no small feat and he is unsure whether Diana can muster the strength for it right now. Either way, there is no time to debate. He nods towards the officer and turns the key to start the car's engine.

Navigating past hundreds of other vehicles lined up in the queue they spent the entire day in, Vitalii tries to remember the next border crossing located further south. The intricacies of martial law remain nebulous and poorly communicated. He clings to a thin sliver of hope that fresh developments or a compassionate border officer might permit him to cross there. The family returns to the same hotel, steeling themselves for another restless night.

At 5am on Sunday, Vitalii and Diana gently stir their three children awake and begin their journey towards the next border crossing in Chop, a mere twenty-five kilometres south. Another long day in the queue awaits them, each moment filled with anxiety and the hope for a more favourable outcome than that of the previous two days.

At this time, all males between the ages of eighteen to sixty require a so-called 'white ticket', proof of their exemption from martial law to leave Ukraine. Since the initial communication was released on 24 February, several amendments have been issued, creating a challenging labyrinth of regulations for us to decipher. We are uncertain of the exact requirements for an official release from military service during wartime, and where these specific documents can be procured. The Telegram channels we follow are awash with conflicting information. Some people recount that an 'invitation' from their foreign employers allowed them to obtain written confirmation of their deregistration from their local 'military registration and enlistment office'. Others claim that they went straight to the border crossing point with the papers they received when they were first conscripted for temporary military service at age eighteen.

The official communication signed by Serhiy Deyneko, Head of Ukraine's State Border Service, exempts men declared unfit to serve, sole caregivers of relatives, single parents, guardians of three or more minors, custodians of children with disabilities, and those who have lost a close relative in a previous anti-terror operation. We are still unsure how many men in our team exactly qualify for these exemptions, but it is clear that it will not be many.

As of this afternoon on Sunday, it seems that our best option is to secure shelters in safe locations within Ukraine, where our team members can remain hidden for as long as necessary.

Our office, located near the vibrant city centre of Lviv, will not serve as a secure shelter if Russia decides to strike western Ukraine again. However, a mere 130 kilometres south of Lviv and a four-hour drive from the border to Poland, Slovakia, and Hungary lies Ivano-Frankivsk, Danylo's hometown. It is home to approximately 240,000 residents, including Danylo's mother, father, and brother.

Ivano-Frankivsk is a serene city with a rich history influenced by its Polish, Austrian, and Soviet eras. It is renowned for its unique blend of architectural styles, spanning from Renaissance and Baroque to Soviet Modernism. The city centre, adorned with cobblestone streets, houses charming coffee shops and hosts the annual Ivano-Frankivsk blacksmith festival, contributing to a vibrant local arts scene. The city is surrounded by beautiful landscapes, enclosed by national parks and the Carpathian Mountains, home to Ukraine's highest peak, Mount Hoverla. Located 650 kilometres from Kyiv and lacking any significant military infrastructure, these rural areas appear to be less likely targets for Russian forces.

Chapter 12

No good time for a holiday

27 February 2022

Unfortunately, the process of finding accommodation for our employees has become even more challenging in the past twenty-four hours. Taking inspiration from online influencers, individuals worldwide have started to use the platform Airbnb as a means to provide financial support to Ukrainians. They book accommodations they never intend to use, effectively directing funds straight into the hands of the hosts. When Airbnb releases data on the initiative a week later, it shows more than 61,000 nights have been booked in Ukraine since the war's onset.

While this new way of giving is well-intentioned, it is not a system designed to reach the most vulnerable or those in poverty. It also poses a significant challenge for us, as properties that are technically vacant are no longer visible or bookable on the platform.

After hours of exhaustive searches across numerous booking platforms, Danylo finds a hotel in Bukovel, a popular ski resort. He promptly books all the available rooms. The large black and white building with a gable roof could provide a temporary home for up to twenty-three of our team members and their families, which is a promising start. We attempt to pay for the booking using multiple credit cards. Every time, we receive an initial confirmation, only for it to be cancelled shortly thereafter. Half an hour later, Danylo succeeds in contacting the hotel directly and learns that they only accept cash payments due to the failures of bank transfers following Russia's invasion.

Foreign currency transactions have been halted due to a moratorium on the banking system imposed under Ukraine's martial law guidelines . Consequently, we urgently need to understand which families wish to stay in Bukovel, estimate their arrival time, and work out a way to provide them with UAH 294,280 in cash. On the call, we shake our heads as we lock eyes and let out deep sighs. Another day, another challenge.

The repercussions of the martial law guidelines are not limited to bank transfers either. They also restrict cash withdrawals from individual accounts to UAH 100,000 per day. Hence, we will need to disburse the accommodation funds to three different employees, each of whom can withdraw this amount from their account and converge at the hotel. Alternatively, we will have to convince the hotel owner to accept staggered payments. It is no easy endeavour, but there has been no easy path for us lately.

The receptionist whom Danylo spoke with also seemed wary of bookings made by males. While the establishment is not in a location of current military relevance, hotels are often repurposed in times of war, being transformed into prisons, detention centres, or negotiation sites between war parties. We communicate the situation to our team via our Telegram channel, requesting that female family members handle the bookings if they decide to relocate to Bukovel. We assure them that we will individually reimburse each family.

While waiting for their responses, I work on arranging transportation to Bukovel for our team members arriving in Lviv or Ivano-Frankivsk by train. Lviv has no shortage of car and bus rentals. A number of them have online reservation systems, but none of my booking attempts seem to be successful. Opting for a more direct approach, I decide to try my luck by phone. I select a well-known rental company that operates across Ukraine, hoping they will be familiar with English-speaking tourists. After five rings, a gruff voice answers the call. I picture a semi-bald man in his sixties, wearing a shawl collar cardigan, hunched over an outdated office chair.

When I inform him of my intention to rent a bus for my team's journey from Lviv to Bukovel in the coming days, he agitatedly responds,

'Don't come. No good time for holiday.'

Momentarily, his response catches me off guard.

'Yes, I know. It's not for a holiday, though. I am trying to help my Ukrainian colleagues relocate,' I counter.

Unmoved, he insists that I watch the news to educate myself about the ongoing conflict, emphasising that while Ukraine is indeed a breathtakingly beautiful country, it is certainly not the ideal time to plan a visit. Despite the abrupt conclusion to the short conversation, I manage to confirm the availability of rental buses before hanging up. I am somewhat deflated by the incomplete task but decide to leave finalising the booking to Danylo once we can confirm our transportation needs.

Meanwhile, several employees have tried to make a booking at the hotel in Bukovel by phone, only to be informed that the rooms are no longer available.

POLYANYTSYA

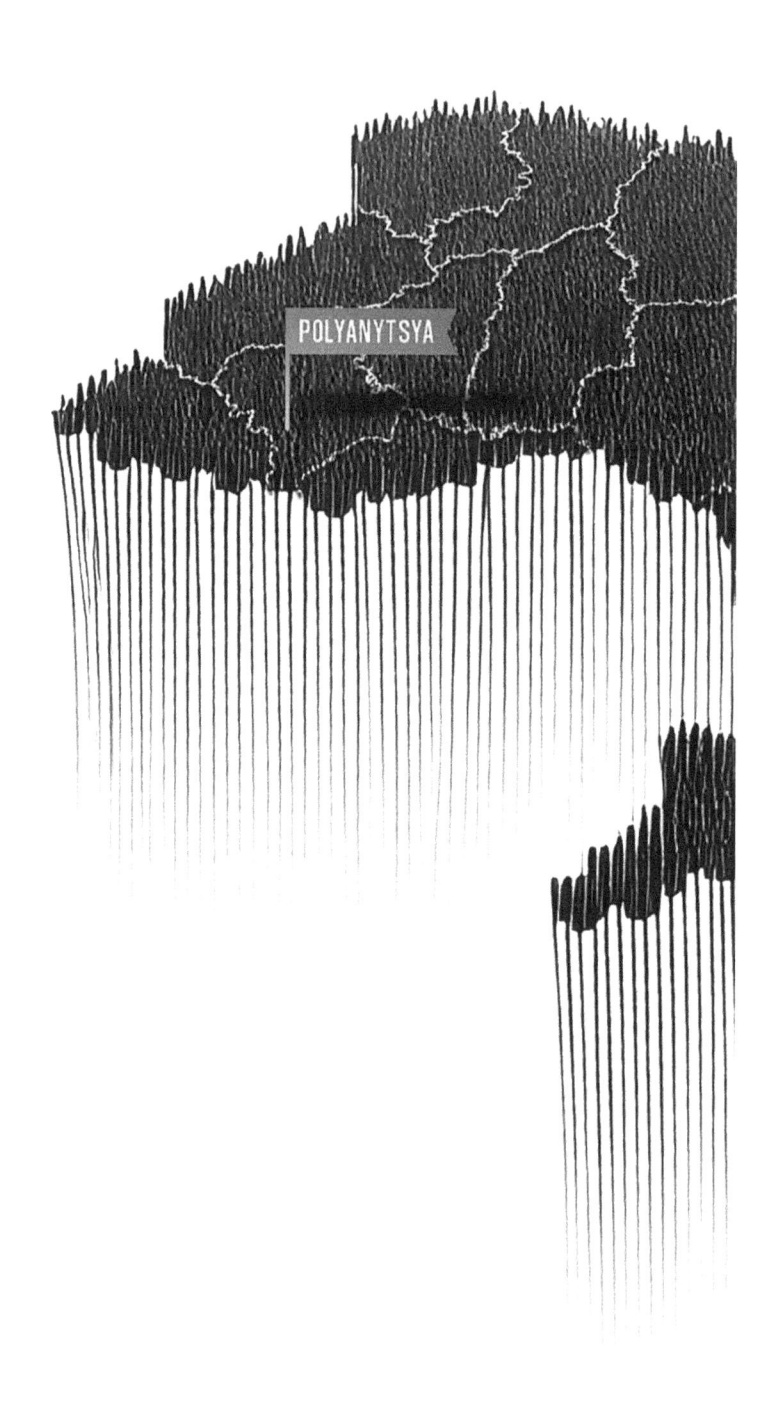

Chapter 13

Yet again, cancelled

27 February 2022

When a message from Vitalii lights up my screen at 7pm, it crystallises the bitter reality that we have wasted half a day on the relentless pursuit to secure accommodation and have absolutely nothing to show for it.

After enduring a thirteen-hour-long queue with three young children and his third thwarted attempt to cross the border further south in Chop, Vitalii finds himself forced to retreat once again. We had hung our hopes on the rumours about 'invitations' from EU employers expediting the process and sent one to Vitalii and all other employees who were weighing the heartrending decision of leaving Ukraine against staying. The signed letters affirmed that we would bear the costs of their relocation and accommodation at their destination.

However, the face of the border guard in Chop remained stern and unimpressed, barring Vitalii's passage without an official statement from an enlistment office. It needed to verify him as a father of three children, all under the age of eighteen, thereby exempting him from military service during wartime.

Now, as every single bed within a 300-kilometre radius from Chop is claimed, Vitalii is forced to grapple with the grim choice between a cold, uncomfortable night spent in the claustrophobic confines of his car or a tiresome journey back to Lviv to sleep in our office.

The sting of failing him gnaws at me, my heart aching with the sharp pang of standing empty-handed. While I will be sleeping in my comfortable bed tonight, I am unable to offer him any viable solution. It is a frustrating and infuriating situation, after having the triumph of securing rooms in Bukovel snatched away earlier. After all, we successfully found and booked accommodation for tonight, yet somehow these beds were given to others.

Hoping this period of hardship will not last much longer, Vitalii and his family prolong their already agonising journey by another four hours, driving back towards Lviv.

We delve back into the seemingly fruitless task of finding safe accommodation to host our colleagues for the coming weeks. Desperation fuels our search now, driving us to sift through every website, every Google search result, regardless of how appalling the photos look or how grim the reviews sound. Anything is better than having families leave their homes in search of refuge, only to end up homeless. Sadly, too many Ukrainian families are forced to endure this cruel fate right now.

Just before the clock strikes midnight, a glimmer of hope breaks through the darkness. Larissa discovers a listing for a holiday home in Polyanytsya on Airbnb. Vacant from 2 March until the first week of April, it is a charming wooden chalet nestled in the mountains. After three failed attempts, the fourth booking goes through. A confirmation email lands in our inbox. We brace ourselves for another cancellation, but none comes. Joy surges through my body, blooming into a profound sense of relief as the tension unravels, and we share a collective sigh of respite.

Despite the chalet's four bedrooms accommodating up to twelve adults, it will not be enough to house everyone. But it is a start, a beacon of hope after this bleak day. We will manage to secure another property the following day, offering shelter for more than thirty people in the mountains of the region Ivano-Frankivsk, safely tucked away from the relentless dread of Russia's omnipresent terror.

Chapter 14

Everything matters

22 February–1 March 2022

For those of us based in Germany, Monday marks the beginning of a focused effort to help our newly arrived colleagues settle in. There is German bureaucracy to be navigated, long-term housing to be secured, foreign customs to be understood and overall, vital moments of normality to be found. It is a complex undertaking for anyone, and an unfair ask of people who have recently escaped a war zone. German authorities remain ill-prepared for the immense influx of refugees arriving in the country, making it incumbent upon our team to ensure that the transition is as smooth as possible.

By this time, more than ten thousand Ukrainians have arrived in Germany. Train stations nationwide, especially in the major cities, are teeming with refugees and volunteers eager to provide a warm welcome and much-needed support. In Berlin, the underground concourse of the central train station has been transformed into a makeshift reception area for refugees. Every day, hundreds, if not thousands, of people line up seeking shelter, food, clothing, SIM cards, and medical aid. They had left everything behind to save their lives, and now they are left with nothing but the dirty clothes on their backs and a single bag that they could carry. They had spent hours, sometimes days, on a journey, determining their destination as they went. Cramped on trains, stacked upon one another, they held their breaths as bombs rained down on their train tracks and roads. They inhaled stale air that had been recycled too many times, air tainted with the smell of sweat, fear, rubble, and blood. They clung to their loved ones and the few belongings they managed to salvage from the lives that had been taken from them. These items often held more emotional than financial or practical value. In the rush to save one's life, where there is no moment to think, the heart dictates the choices. They feel dirty, cold, and exhausted, and yearn for their own beds in homes that no longer exist, in communities that have vanished. Lives they have painstakingly built over decades existed on Wednesday, only to be obliterated on Thursday.

Clothes and shoes are neatly stacked against a wall, organised by gender and age. Beside them, boxes upon boxes of donated items await sorting and distribution. Hundreds of handwritten signs and posters have turned the central train station into a sea of blue and yellow, the colours of the Ukrainian flag. Standing out against the vivid backdrop are volunteers in high-visibility yellow vests. Their name tags specify the languages they speak, and they are eager to assist anyone in need by handing out coffee, food, leaflets, and valuable advice.

A few hundred kilometres away, our company has its own small support team at our headquarters. Svetlana, our Operations Manager, is an unassuming yet enthusiastic organiser. She thrives in coordinating local registrations, providing advice on the essentials of daily life, and translating for our newly migrated colleagues. As an expatriate who moved to the town from Russia in 2012, she has a unique understanding of the challenges faced by our Ukrainian colleagues.

Svetlana emanates an air of serene confidence that defies her petite stature. Her long brown hair, usually worn loose, cascades over her shoulders and features natural blonde streaks that gleam in the sunlight. Her expressive face is almost always illuminated by a warm smile, a testament to her generous spirit. We cherish her for her kind heart and genuine effort to make everyone around her feel at ease.

She had already harboured bleak expectations following Russia's government meeting on 22 February, during which they declared eastern Ukraine to be part of Russia. The notion that Russian troops might invade seemed unthinkable, yet in light of the events of 2014, she knew better. Vladimir Putin was neither bound by international norms nor constrained by what most people would consider sane or reasonable.

On 23 February, she awoke to the darkest of mornings, her eyelids so heavy she could barely lift them. It was as if an iron blanket anchored her to the bed. Even the smallest movement sapped her of her remaining energy. Finally managing to grab her phone from her bedside table, she sent a message excusing herself from work, then locked her phone and pulled the blanket over her head. Consumed by exhaustion, she succumbed to a wave of deep sleep. Hours later, she woke up drowsy and disoriented, uncertain of the time. She remained in this state for the entire day and night, haunted by the foreboding of events that would soon shock the world.

The events of 24 February remained unknown to her until her phone's alarm sounded at 8.30am, and her screen revealed a message from a friend in St. Petersburg: 'These bastards are bombing Ukraine.'

Still wearing the same pyjamas she had put on two days prior, she stared at the message in disbelief. Moments later, shaking off the paralysis it had induced, she walked over to her work desk and opened her laptop. Her fingers trembled as she typed 'meduza.io' into her browser. The independent news outlet, founded in Latvia in 2014, had been her go-to source for reliable information on Russia for years. She could not believe what she saw. Photos and video footage of the bombardment across Ukraine and chilling headlines blurred as her eyes brimmed with tears. She read the headlines again and again, each word piercing deeper than the last. Her left hand rested on her chest as if she was trying to remind herself to breathe. Svetlana remained captive to the heart-wrenching news. For minutes, she oscillated between crying and reading, unable to tear herself away.

Her heart plummeted at the thought of a colleague, whom she had seen in the office less than a week ago. They had caught up over a cup of tea last Friday, and she was set to leave for Kharkiv the following day. Svetlana had cautioned her against flying, feeling deep in her bones that danger was imminent. She texted her but the message remained undelivered. Was she in a bomb shelter underground, or had she been injured by one of the many rockets currently raining down on Kharkiv? The uncertainty was agonising. Finally, after what felt like an eternity, a single tick appeared next to her message in the Telegram app, indicating that it had at last reached the recipient. Yet it remained unread, and it would be hours before she received a response, leaving her fraught with anxiety and dread.

She continued reaching out to other friends across Ukraine. Some were already fleeing westward, unsure of their destination but instinctively seeking refuge from the unyielding Russian assault that had commenced just hours earlier. However, the majority had no plans to leave their country. Despite the grim circumstances, they were determined to stay, to support their homeland in any way possible, and to continue their lives even though those lives would be dramatically changed.

By midday, Svetlana finally mustered the clarity of thought and strength to nourish her body with a shower and some food. She avoided looking in the bathroom mirror, fearful of the reflection that might confront her.

'In times of crisis, everyone's got to do what they can do best to help,' she whispered to herself. 'You've got to pull yourself together now.' Upon receiving the Google Meet link from Larissa, she joined the call and began researching buses for our evacuation plan.

As the day wore on, she felt the iron blanket, which she had struggled so valiantly to cast off that morning, envelop her once more. She returned to bed, overwhelmed by guilt. The weight of her panic seemed to rest solely on her shoulders: Why had this happened? What could she have done to prevent it? When would it stop?

The events of the past few hours had fundamentally altered how she felt about being a Russian citizen. She sensed that the world would now view her differently, and she herself felt guilty on account of her heritage. What did it mean to be a Russian citizen now? What did it make her—a victim, a follower, a bystander, or a perpetrator?

Though she had never been a supporter of Putin, she had not vocally opposed him either. Raising one's voice against the power corridors of the Kremlin was not a simple act of defiance. Rather, it was a decision that could attract a whirlwind of repercussions, including arrest and imprisonment. Livelihoods were on the line, too; speaking out might cost one their job. Online activities were closely monitored, with every post, comment, or 'like' under scrutiny, making one a target for internet trolls. Putin ensured that the consequences of opposing him were dire for oneself and one's family, who often became collateral victims of a decision to dissent.

On Friday, 25 February 2022, she went straight from her bed to her laptop. After a sleepless night haunted by harrowing images, she tried to distract herself with tasks, but even the simplest ones felt insurmountable. Images of bombed towns and train stations overflowing with refugees pursued her relentlessly. Her questions remained unanswered, her pleas for an end to the violence unheard. She remained mired in guilt for what had already occurred and gripped by fear of what was yet to come.

Facing her Ukrainian colleagues presented a unique challenge as well. How could she convey her profound regret and sympathy for what was happening to their country and their people when words seemed so inadequate and disingenuous coming from a Russian citizen? If she felt this way herself, how could she expect them to react differently? The fear of rejection loomed large, and she found it difficult to trust that their pre-existing relationships would outweigh any animosity they might feel towards her for her Russian background, especially considering her own conflicted feelings. So she chose to maintain a distance.

She spent the remainder of Friday and her entire weekend assisting a friend with collecting supplies for Ukrainian medical professionals. The charitable project had been initiated within hours and proved enormously successful. By Sunday, more than ten tons of donations had been dropped off, all of which needed to be organised and prepared for delivery. Svetlana devoted every spare moment to supporting charities and helping Larissa prepare the boxes for our first arrivals on Sunday evening. These activities provided a much-needed respite from her overwhelming thoughts and emotions. For a Russian citizen though, they came at a steep price. By the end of the week, her charitable efforts would be tantamount to a criminal offence punishable by up to ten years in prison in Russia. Supporting those whom Putin considered enemies was not a trivial offence.

We had not seen Svetlana on the call for four days and were seriously worried. We had not missed the emotional toll that the past days had taken on her.

'How's she doing?', Danylo asked Larissa on the call.

'I saw her on Saturday while we were preparing the packages for Serhiy's arrival,' she responded. 'She seemed somewhat better but she's still having a tough time.'

That same day, Danylo and I both reached out to Svetlana. Danylo's message stirred more emotions in her. Here was a Ukrainian man, himself reeling with the grief of watching his country brutally invaded, extending a hand to someone he could perceive as the enemy. Overwhelmed by guilt, she couldn't bring herself to respond for several days.

It was hard to miss the toll that the past days had taken on her. Her usual positivity had been replaced by a rare seriousness I had never seen in her. She tried to maintain her composure, but could not conceal the fatigue and sorrow her body radiated. It broke my heart to hear how much guilt she was shouldering, and I wished I could absolve her of it. None of us would have burdened her with this weight.

By this point, debates over the responsibility of Russian citizens were heating conversations one could overhear in restaurants, on trains, and over the radio. Many people were hoping that Russia's citizenry would rise against Putin's invasion. There was anticipation for public demonstrations, for change, albeit tinged with concerns about the inevitable pain and sacrifice such actions would entail. However, days had passed, and while Western media were not entirely clued in on the situation within Russia, signs of protest remained scarce.

Like so many people with ties to Russia around the world, Svetlana found maintaining relationships with Russian friends and family increasingly difficult. Influenced by the one-sided media coverage in their country, many subscribed to Putin's narrative that Russian forces were liberating Ukraine. These divergent realities led to heated disagreements, with too much at stake for either side to yield. It seemed best to avoid mentioning the war altogether unless one was prepared to create an irrevocable rift. On both sides of the border, the war was splitting families in so many ways.

Every day was a delicate act of trying to create moments of normality amid the unpredictability of the unfolding nightmare. This Monday, a simple walk home from the supermarket through her tranquil town ends with a heart-wrenching phone call from a friend in Ukraine. They have been friends for years, first meeting at a language course in Germany. Both a little shy and navigating unfamiliar terrain, their eyes met, smiles were exchanged, and a sense of comfort was immediately established between them. After her friend moved back to Ukraine for work, they kept in touch through regular phone calls, usually on Mondays. But this call is unlike any other.

A few minutes into their conversation, Svetlana hears Kyiv's air raid sirens blaring in the background. Her friend hurriedly takes cover under her kitchen table, the room with the sturdiest walls in her apartment. An unsettling silence follows, interrupted only by faint breaths. From over 1,500 kilometres away, Svetlana can hear the bombs drawing closer. It terrifies her.

Almost unconsciously, she finds herself leaning against the nearest wall of her one-bedroom apartment, sliding down to crouch on the floor, her head bowed heavily onto her knees. Tears cloud her vision. Neither says a word. She hears her friend's breaths grow heavier, punctuated by the chattering of her teeth, her body quivering with fear. They both realise that these could be the last minutes they would ever share.

Svetlana is choked with emotion, her words stuck in her throat. All she can manage to whisper is, 'I love you. I hope you stay alive.'

They fall silent again. About fifteen minutes later, the surrounding noise starts to fade. 'Sveta, I think it's over,' her friend mumbles cautiously, her voice tinged with relief. 'I survived.'

Tuesday, 1 March 2022 commences with a burst of activity aimed at helping our first arrivals get settled. Svetlana assists them in officially registering with authorities, a mandatory bureaucratic procedure that every new resident in Germany must complete within three days of arrival. She noticed how exhausted Larissa was on Saturday after several consecutive days on the call with us and managing on just a few hours of sleep. Caring for her gives Svetlana the push she needs to overcome her apprehensions about interacting with Ukrainians.

She makes a point of disclosing her Russian heritage to everyone she meets upfront, feeling a need for transparency about a facet of her identity that, just a few days earlier, would have seemed of little relevance. It is an attempt to preempt the rejection she so deeply fears. But not a single person reproaches her.

For weeks and months, Svetlana wrestles with her level of moral responsibility, her own complicity, and the subtleties that differentiate followers from bystanders. Even as she does everything in her power to support Ukraine now, she cannot help but blame herself for not protesting against her own government earlier. Her family had seemed detached, almost aloof from the issue. They knew that the news in their country was skewed, that their government was corrupt, and that Putin was a dangerous man. Yet distancing themselves from these uncomfortable truths, they went about their daily lives in relative peace. After all, it is easy to become accustomed to our environment. How many of us actively question what is happening on a larger scale in our countries?

24 February 2022 changed everything for her. The day instilled a pain that became her constant companion, one that takes a full year to begin to subside. She understood that every single moment we spend silently observing may have more impact than we realise, and is irreversible.

Every decision to take action makes a difference. Every choice to do nothing counts. While life speeds by so quickly that we struggle to take it all in, everything matters.

IVANO-FRANKIVSK

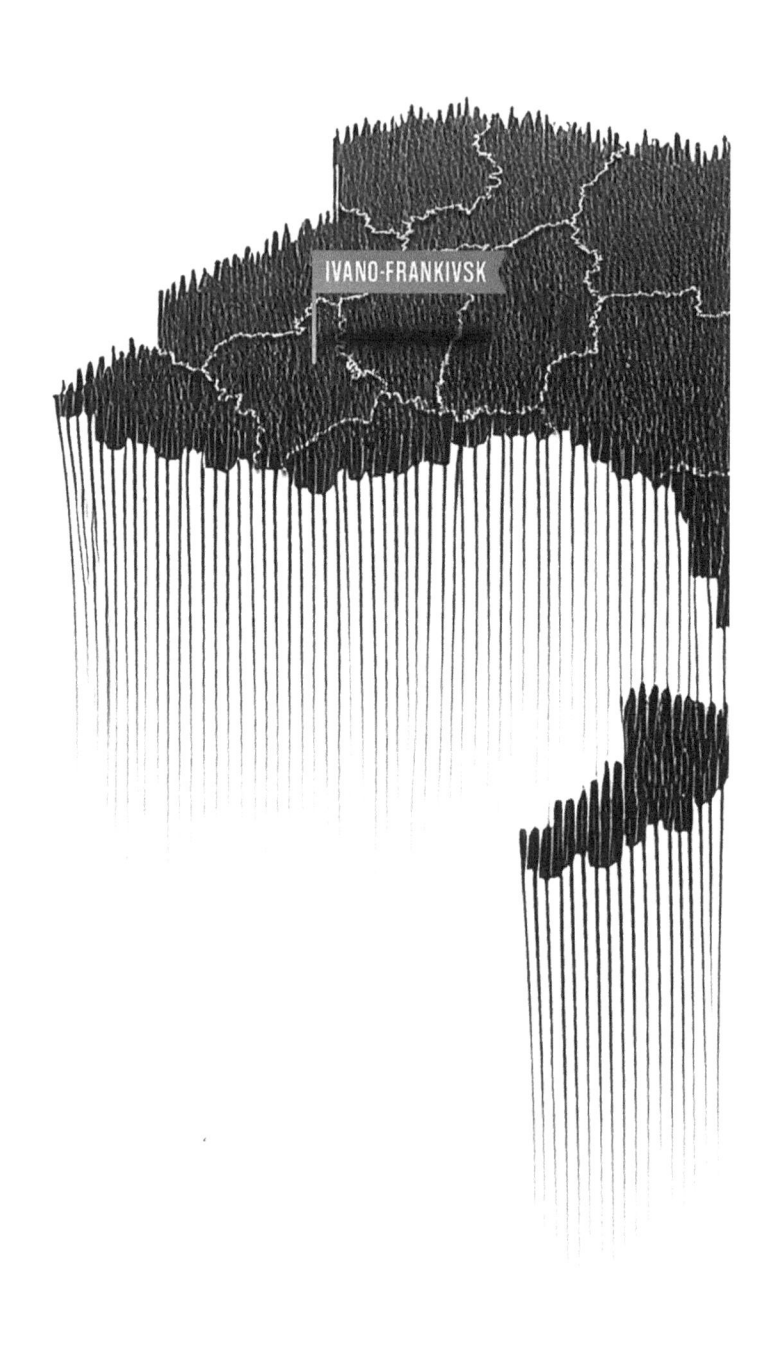

Chapter 15

One hell of a Monday

28 February 2022

A reminder from my calendar punctuates the morning—it is 9am, almost time for the daily meeting with my project team. Amid the ongoing tumult, days blur into one another, forming a continuous sequence of events. We have been communicating continuously with our Ukrainian team since Thursday, but unfortunately have missed doing the same with our colleagues spread out across other parts of Europe.

Thirty minutes later, I am on Zoom, face-to-face with my team. Their expressions reveal a blend of curiosity, anxiety, and uncertainty. It is a new and complex situation for all of us to navigate. They are conflicted about whether to offer uplifting words or discuss the tragic events of recent days and the disheartening absence of any foreseeable resolution. Is it inappropriate to focus on work at such a time, or irresponsible not to, given that projects are what fund our rescue initiatives? One of them is German, another Irish, and another Russian. I am trying to acknowledge their individual experiences and the varied ways in which they are coping with this crisis.

We discuss Ukraine's application to join the European Union, the imminent first round of ceasefire talks expected for today, and our collective scepticism about any short-term relief these developments might bring for Ukraine's people. I share stories of colleagues who have managed to escape from the volatile regions in the east and those who are planning to relocate to Germany. Lastly, I bring up the recent arrival of Serhiy and Vlad. I try to be honest and transparent but opt to omit the stark realities faced by many of our colleagues stranded in the east. I promise to keep them updated on any critical developments. The unpredictable nature of this war will call for many spur-of-the-moment decisions in the coming days and weeks, such as choosing when to communicate, what to share, how to verify the reliability of our information sources, and how to honour our company's value of transparency without further traumatising our teams.

In the afternoon, I commence my daily check-ins with our Ukrainian employees. While we mostly communicate via individual chats on Telegram, we have also set up a new central email address for inquiries, aptly named 'fuckputin'. Despite the hardship and terrors we have witnessed in the past week, we have maintained our sense of humour. I had hoped to establish a form of routine around these daily check-ins, but today feels even more challenging than the very first time last Friday.

The military convoy on the outskirts of Ukraine's capital, Kyiv, now stretches more than forty kilometres and continues to expand. This morning, Russia attacked Kharkiv, launching grad rockets into three residential neighbourhoods. The country's second largest city is home to 1.5 million people, including three employees I need to contact.

Nighttime and early morning shelling has become a horrifyingly regular occurrence, and most cities have imposed a curfew from 10pm to 8am. During daylight hours, people venture out of their shelters to secure essentials such as water, food, and medical supplies, and to soak in some much-needed daylight and fresh air. This morning's attack caught the residents of Kharkiv off guard. According to news reports and information from Telegram channels, the number of civilian casualties remains uncertain. I try to avoid contemplating the possibility that any of our team or their families could be among them, but I know that any lack of response to my messages will trigger a cascade of haunting images in my mind, the kind that often creeps up on me these days when I foolishly lower my guard.

After staring at my draft message for a good thirty minutes and inventing reasons for delays, I finally press 'send'. Minutes feel like hours, and hours like days. The silence is tormenting. Danylo is on the call with me, awaiting responses from his list of colleagues. To distract ourselves, we engage in mundane tasks like double-checking employee data on our Notion platform and designing a company logo in Ukraine's national colours for our public communications.

Three hours later, my phone is finally buzzing with the first replies. Their stories are heart-wrenching, but everyone is safe for now. Life in Kharkiv and Kyiv has been confined to basements and bunkers, crammed into tiny spaces allowing little more than two square metres per person. Seated on benches, their backs pressed against the wall and their legs cloaked in blankets to withstand the freezing temperatures underground, they wait. During the city-wide curfew, the bunkers become even more crowded. Food is passed around and shared. Adults read, debate, and pray, while children entertain themselves with games of 'hide-and-seek' and books. With belongings pared down to the bare minimum, toys have become a luxury.

I tell them about our humour-infused new email address, my amusing yet failed attempt to book a bus in Lviv, and the safe shelters in the mountains that we have just secured. In the face of the relentless hardship that pervades their every minute, all I can offer as consolation is a sliver of positive news. I am hoping that our conversations, limited to messaging and rarely lasting longer than a few minutes, are a beacon of light in their bleak routine. In turn, knowing that they are unharmed is the highlight of my days.

Around 7.30pm, our Google Meet call grows quiet except for Danylo and me. Larissa is taking a short break to have dinner, and Olena is taking care of her children. Today, I can barely recall what we have talked about, or if we engaged in much conversation at all. The moments before and after have faded into obscurity, eclipsed by the ensuing longest minutes of these seven days and seven nights.

Danylo's phone is buzzing. Initially, I barely pay attention to it. Given his role as the primary contact for all communications in our company's Telegram channel, it happens almost every minute. However, a sudden twitch in my chest tells me that this time is different. He stares at his phone.

'My brother says the air raid sirens have gone off in Ivano-Frankivsk. They are about to shell my town,' he says.

I open my mouth but no words come out. My heart sinks. Time comes to a standstill. I try to maintain eye contact with him across our screens. Remain calm. Stay strong. Offer support. But I am at a loss for what to do. We lapse into silence. It feels as if the world has been muted. Neither of us dares to breathe. We both sit there, frozen, waiting for each tortuous second to crawl by. I wish I could teleport myself to Delft.

I do not need to picture my family huddled in our basement to feel his anguish. The helplessness. The vulnerability. The despair. I do not know how he manages not to crumble under its weight.

Several minutes later, Danylo's phone vibrates again. We lock eyes. It could be a message indicating that the shelling has stopped. Or that someone has been wounded. Or something even worse. He inhales deeply and taps on the notification.

'It's over,' he says. 'They're okay.'

That evening, the haunting sound of air raid sirens echoed through six districts of Ivano-Frankivsk Oblast for an agonising one hour and fifty-seven minutes. Thousands of people spent them confined within shelters and basements, and equally as many anxiously awaiting news from their loved ones. For a few moments, I became his companion in the hell that so many Ukrainians endure every single day.

Chapter 16

Tides of fear and reverence

29 February–3 March 2022

It is Tuesday. My Telegram is inundated with images of families crammed into cars, chairs lined up in crowded bunkers, and volunteers radiating pride as they stand in front of defensive walls of sandbags. The latest message arrives from Dimitri, a Belarussian developer living in Kyiv with his Ukrainian girlfriend. Initially, he had reached out to me through a mutual friend in Berlin, seeking help to evacuate from Kyiv, but eventually, he chose to stay and fight for Ukraine. The photo that he sent depicts him smiling confidently into the camera, a glass bottle clasped in his hand. As he explains in the text message, he has just crafted his very first Molotov Cocktail from scratch. It is arguably the world's most infamous firebomb and one that originated in Soviet conflicts. As much as I admire Dimitri's bravery, my earnest hope is that other nations will supply them with far superior arms than this soon.

In Rzeszów, Farid experiences his first morning of restful slumber since his arrival. The emotional turmoil of the past few days has left him drained, but deciding on a course of action on Sunday has reinvigorated him. He now has a plan for the coming days. After sharing his ambitious ideas with family, friends, and our company's CEO, they have agreed to transfer almost 10,000 Euro to his bank account within the next forty-eight hours. As soon as his bags are packed, he will visit the numerous military shops scattered around

Rzeszów. There, he'll acquire as much defensive and protective equipment as his budget and the space in his vehicle can accommodate. At predetermined meeting points, he will meet with contacts recommended by his Ukrainian friends who are on their way to Ukraine. They will take the material across the border and deliver it to his friends who have enlisted in the army or local defence forces. Several drivers have been organised for the coming days, so Farid is planning to buy as much material as his funds will allow.

His exploratory walks around the city have proven beneficial as well. During one such stroll yesterday, he shared his plan with a young Polish man he encountered, who immediately pointed Farid towards military shops he believed would be most useful for his mission.

By 11am, Farid zips up his duffel bag and closes the door to his hotel room door behind him. He leaves the key card with the receptionist, wishing him farewell. Based on his research, there are five military shops near Rzeszów, and he intends to start with those recommended by his new Polish friend. A variety of stores sell military-related equipment, gear, and clothing in Poland, typically surplus goods from the Polish military. His first destination is a mere six-minute drive away.

His heart pounds heavily as he strides confidently through the door of the army store. He has visited this kind of shop before to purchase clothes and minor supplies, but never with the intention of taking them to the front lines of a war. He has never held a shopping list in his hands with the express purpose of ensuring the survival of people he knows personally. He pulls the list from his pocket; it includes the items that Larissa and I sent him last Sunday, along with instructions from his friends in Lviv.

At first glance, the shop is overwhelming. Items are packed from floor to ceiling, with racks extending from every wall and overhead, holding an array of vests and jackets in black, green, and camouflage colours, their prices handwritten on tags. As he navigates through the shop, he almost stumbles over boxes of knee protection gear strewn on the floor. The rack he passes is laden with warm clothing—pullovers and pants with more pockets than he can count. He reaches out to touch the lining of one of the sleeves, the soft padding feeling thick and warm beneath his fingers. It feels like it might suffice for Ukraine's freezing temperatures for a short period, but probably not for extended hours in a trench. Above the rack stands a mannequin, dressed in full uniform. The sight prompts an involuntary mental image of Victor and Iurii clad in the same outfit, the reality of his task hitting home once more.

The shop appears to offer a wide range of sizes for most clothes, from small to extra-large. Realising that he has forgotten to inquire about sizes, he decides that 'large' should suffice for most of the men he knows. As he examines the thick boots stacked against the back wall, he finds the gloves specified on his list and grabs ten pairs of the flame-resistant variety the store has on hand. They will provide an enhanced grip when handling weapons and tools, and offer camouflage and protection against the vibration when operating heavy machinery.

Next on his list are magazine carriers, pouches that hold and feed ammunition to firearms. He follows a sign towards a back room, taking note of the walls painted in shades of green, white, and brown to reflect the military theme. The plaster is peeling and most of the walls are lined with clothes and bags, a distraction from the worn-out decor.

Just beyond the makeshift changing rooms, delineated by long black curtains, he locates what appears to be the pouch section. He picks up the topmost item. The compact, olive green bag is made of durable canvas and partitioned into several individual compartments, each secured by a cover flap that fastens with snaps. It exudes a distinct Eastern European military aesthetic. He pulls the long strap over his shoulder to try it on. This model also comes with a belt clip for attachment to a tactical vest, the next item on his list.

The store offers splinter protection vests in olive, black, and military camouflage. These vests are designed to shield the wearer from projectiles and fragments resulting from explosions or shrapnel. He decides to take as many as he can feasibly carry back to the car. As he lightly traces his fingers over the rough worn belt of the vest, a sudden wave of fear engulfs him. What are the chances of a bullet striking this very vest? What if this vest, the one he is buying to protect his friends, fails to shield Victor or Iurii? What if he never sees his friends again? He quickly shakes his head, trying to dispel the unsettling thought.

A short man with cropped hair and a military jacket stands behind the counter. He has a strong jawline and distinctive facial features. His soft blue eyes offer a stark contrast to his dark beard and thick eyebrows. He appears to be in excellent shape, and his demeanour carries a certain solemnity and seriousness. Spotting the unit insignia on his jacket, Farid surmises that he must be a veteran. He is engaged in a heated discussion with another customer in Polish. Not being fluent in the language, Farid can only discern the word 'Ukraina'–Ukraine. Farid clears his throat to get the man's attention, and the cashier turns around to face him.

'That's a lot of military gear,' the man observes, his gaze sweeping over the items. 'Are you going to Ukraine?'

'Yes,' Farid affirms.

For a fleeting moment, they make eye contact, an unspoken understanding passing between them as they exchange a serious nod.

'Good luck,' the man says succinctly, scanning the last item.

'Thank you,' Farid replies as confidently as he can manage.

With more than 3,000 Euros spent from his own budget and his account almost empty, Farid steps out of the store. The splinter vests cost 100 Euro each, roughly twice the price suggested by the young Polish man he met on Sunday. The rising demand must have inflated the prices already, and by the time he returns two days later, the cost will have soared to 800 euros.

He adopts the same approach at the next shop, quickly referencing his list as he steps inside, then mentally ticking off items as he gathers the required quantity, plus a few extras. While he does so swiftly, he finds it hard to disconnect the items from the racing thoughts about who might end up wearing them, the places where they will be taken, and what might happen when they arrive.

Farid opts for the most expensive tactical glasses the store carries. They come with multiple lens colours to enhance visual clarity, and are made from high-impact materials—both features that he feels will be essential in combat. Farid ticks helmets, shovels, and knee and elbow protectors off his list as he hauls his selections to the counter. His steps are slow and weighted. He fights off the thought of one of his friends donning this gear in the coming weeks. As a fervent military enthusiast, he knows all too well that these helmets, while offering protection against small arms fire, will stand no chance against a high-velocity rifle or armour-piercing projectiles.

As Farid walks to his car, he briefly closes his eyes, attempting to recall the remaining items on the list: sleeping bags, nutrition packs, and medical supplies. He decides to secure these items tomorrow. Even without these final pieces, his blue Audi is packed to the brim and he has agreed to meet with the first driver in half an hour.

Getting into the car, he grips the steering wheel firmly, taking a deep breath. For the first time in days, he can sense lightness and determination in his body. Delivering these supplies makes him feel in control, and helps him shake off the oppressive feelings of despair and overwhelm that have haunted him since Thursday. The newfound mission provides him with purpose and much-needed tasks to focus on.

He marvels at Ukraine's resistance and his friends' courage, feeling honoured to do his part. A part of him still debates whether he should also volunteer in the army, a thought his friends and family have tried to dissuade him from over the past few days, but one that keeps nudging at him the closer he gets to the border. Ukraine had welcomed him warmly. His friends had opened their homes to him, and their families have embraced him as one of their own. He wrestles with the question of whether anything, even volunteering at the front line, will ever alleviate his nagging sensation of not doing enough.

Fifteen minutes later, he stops at the agreed rest station and takes out his phone to refresh his memory on the make of the car and the number plate he was looking for. Shortly afterwards, a white Sprinter van pulls in. Farid subtly signals the driver with his hand.

'Piotr?' he asks as the driver's door swings open.

'Yes. You must be Farid. Is everything ready?'

As he gets out of the van, Piotr stands at about 1.90 metres tall. He is wearing worn-out jeans, sturdy boots, and a thick, faded blue hoodie. His broad, squared shoulders exhibit an undeniable strength, one that speaks more of practicality than vanity. His hair, a grizzled mix of black and silver, is slightly dishevelled, a choice that seems less about style and more a reflection of his indifference. A dense, trimmed beard covers most of his face. His piercing blue eyes, framed by weathered lines and bushy eyebrows, carry a certain depth as they seek to lock eyes with Farid.

'Yeah, all the supplies are securely packed in the trunk. I've done my best to organise them for easy transport.'

'Great, let's transfer them to my van.'

As they begin moving the boxes from Farid's car into Piotr's van, which is already laden with boxes, Farid's curiosity about Piotr's motives peaks.

'I appreciate your help with this, Piotr.'

'No need to thank me. We're all doing what we can.' Piotr responds gently.

'Have you done this sort of thing before? I mean, is this your first time crossing the border since last Thursday?'

Pietro sighs, 'No, I hadn't before Thursday. But I've made deliveries daily since then.'

'I see. Thanks for your courage. I live in Lviv and plan to return, but I have to sort out a few matters back home in Germany first.'

Piotr nods sympathetically. 'I wish you luck. Alright, everything's loaded. I should get going.'

'Best of luck to you, too, Piotr. And once again, thank you.'

Piotr jumps back into the van and drives away. Farid lingers for a few moments, watching him merge onto the highway, silently hoping all the equipment will safely reach Lviv. Then he returns to his car and drives back to the hotel. It has been an exhausting but gratifying day. Certainly not a bad start. Four hours later, he receives a message from Iurii that Piotr made it to Lviv. Crossing the border took longer than expected. Traffic slowly inched forward in both directions, forming a lengthy serpent of vehicles. Given the slow progress of official military aid from other countries, Ukrainians are clearly determined to source as much equipment as they possibly can from Poland.

The next morning, Farid leaves the hotel in search of the remaining items on his list. To his surprise, the military shop he pulls up to first is bustling with activity. People are eagerly walking in and out, loading their vehicles with large cardboard boxes of supplies. He is taken aback by the number of women involved; the crowd is almost an even split between males and females. Inside, he finds most of the shelves empty. The walls behind the cashier's counter bear empty boxes previously holding guns, knives, and projectiles—items typically locked away in such stores to prevent theft and adhere to licensing requirements.

He spots a man who appears to be a shop assistant and inquires about the availability of further supplies.

'You're too late. We've been swamped in the past few days. Within a 200-kilometre radius from the border, you'll have no luck finding more military equipment at the moment,' the assistant replies.

Farid stands still, momentarily stunned, before a chuckle escapes him. His hand instinctively moves to his chest, covering his heart as he grapples with the surge of conflicting emotions that consume him. Part of him wants to weep with indignation about the injustice that led to this point, and for the countless lives that will inevitably be lost in this war. Yet he cannot help grinning, inspired by the Ukrainians' resilience and awe. Faced with a seemingly insurmountable task, they have taken matters into their own hands, mobilising every resource and individual they have.

A friendly stranger, having overheard the conversation, turns to him.

'What are you looking for?' he asks.

'Sleeping bags, nutritional packs, and some medical supplies,' Farid replies.

'There's a camping store and a large pharmacy not too far from here. They still had supplies when I visited yesterday. Let me show you on Google Maps.'

Farid thanks him and immediately heads to the indicated locations. He manages to acquire the last remaining sleeping bags and nutritional packs from the camping store and most of the medical supplies he needs from the pharmacy.

For two more days, he continues his mission, purchasing equipment and coordinating with designated drivers bound for Ukraine. Almost 10,000 Euro, a collective contribution from his friends and family and our company, have accumulated in his bank account by now. He is determined to utilise every cent with the utmost efficacy.

Heeding the concerned calls from friends and family back in Germany, he decides to return home for a few weeks to assure them that he has indeed emerged safely from Ukraine and that there is no cause for alarm. However, Farid is certain that it will not be long before he finds himself back in what he has started to consider his new home.

While he is away, the situation across Ukraine deteriorates. Kyiv, Kherson, and Mariupol find themselves under heavy bombardment. The Mariupol Drama Theatre, which is being used as a shelter by civilians, is bombed by Russian forces, killing an estimated 300 people and leaving the city in a humanitarian crisis.

Many residents from other parts of Ukraine flee to Lviv, seeking safety from the conflict. On busy days, Lviv's train station alone welcomes 60,000 people, many of them arriving exhausted and confused. The city's infrastructure, including schools and kindergartens, is repurposed to accommodate the influx of people. Volunteers and local organisations provide assistance, including food, shelter, medical aid, and psychological support.

On 13 March, Lviv itself experiences its first attacks since the invasion started. Russian forces launch an airstrike on the Yavoriv military range just outside the city, killing 35 people and injuring 134 others. Five days later, four missiles hit the Lviv State Aircraft Repair plant.

Farid's car with the equipment he bought in Poland, February 2022

A PHOTO OF THE EQUIPMENT, TAKEN THE NIGHT OF THE HANDOVER,
FEBRUARY 2022

LVIV

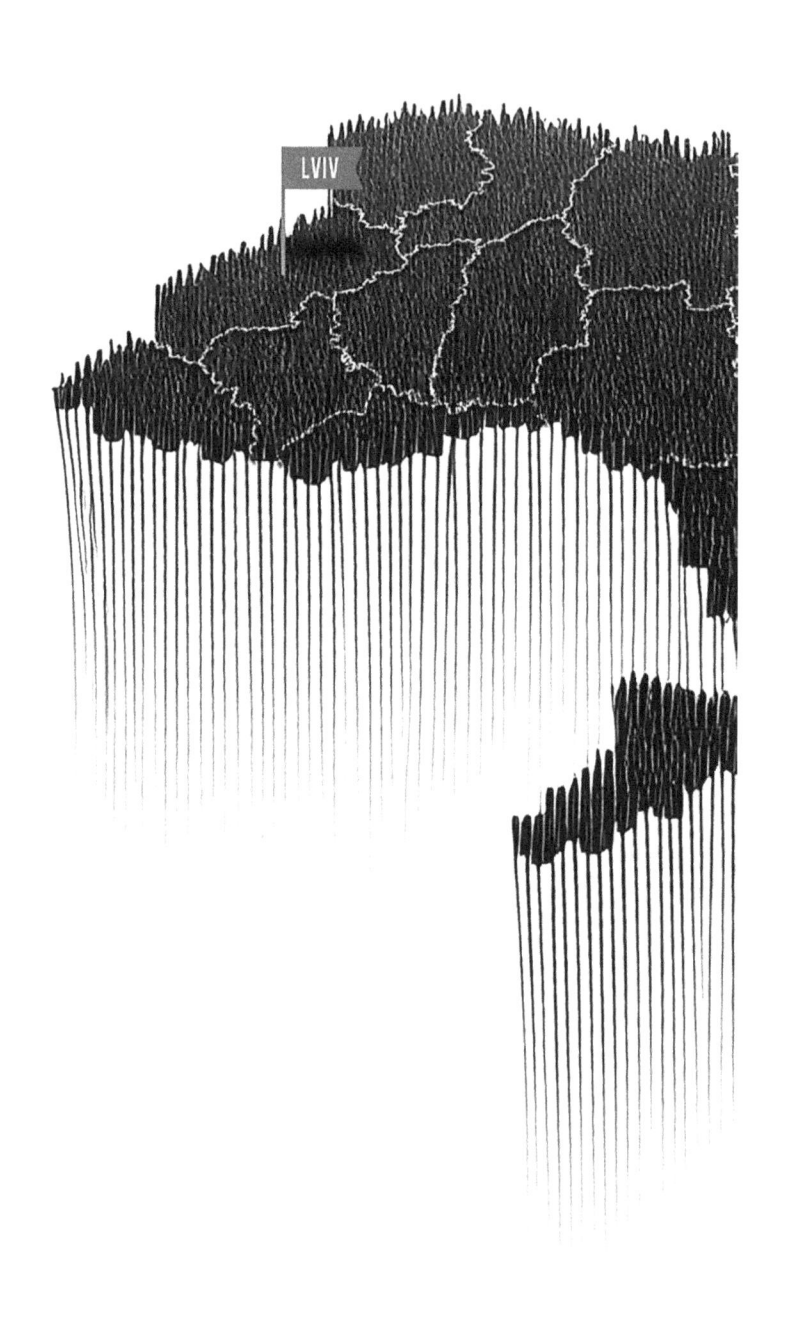

Chapter 17

Lviv, you've changed

25 March–19 April 2022

Four weeks after he left Lviv, Farid is on his way back with his last load of supplies. The Korczowa-Krakowiec border crossing into Ukraine is more congested than he expected. After two hours in line, he finally approaches the checkpoint, and the inspection process is slow and thorough. Ukrainians have grown more suspicious of potential Russian infiltrators crossing the border to launch internal attacks. They have witnessed this tactic before during the Crimea conflict in 2014.

Farid feels his heartbeat intensify as he carefully navigates the highway towards Lviv. Though Lviv has not suffered any missile attacks since 24 February, he is unsure how safe the city is right now, dreading the three-kilometre stretch flanking the train tracks, which he has already passed three times on his way out of Ukraine. The lanes heading toward the Polish border continue to be congested with Ukrainians fleeing the encroaching Russian aggression.

The speakers fill the car with melodies from his favourite Spotify playlist of Ukrainian songs, carefully curated by him and his friends a few months ago. He turns up the volume for the remainder of his drive, humming along to the familiar tunes.

As the minutes tick by, the anticipation that Farid felt when crossing the border gradually gives way to a weight in his chest. The sobering realisation dawns on him that this might be the last time he sees his friends before they depart for the training camp, a stepping stone to their impending military service. Since 24 February 2022, tens of thousands of Ukrainians have stepped forward to volunteer for the army, resulting in an extensive waiting list for individuals ready to be summoned for training. Iurii and Vlad have not received their calls yet, but with each passing day, the odds increase that their summons could arrive at any moment.

Farid wonders how they will maintain contact. At the moment, he struggles to think of any appropriate words to say to someone who is gearing up to fight in a war for their country. How frequently should he call them? How can he offer support on difficult days, which will undoubtedly be most of them? What will they talk about? No trouble he is going through can ever measure up to the immense daily burden they will bear. Discussing mundane matters seems almost disrespectful. Then again, they might be craving a distraction from their arduous and monotonous daily routines. He knows his friends well by now; the last thing they would want is pity. But the line between pity and compassion is a fine one, and he will struggle not to cross it in their eyes.

One hour and forty minutes later, Farid parks in the office parking space, turns off the ignition, and applies the handbrake. He leaves everything in the car for the moment, keen to reunite with his friends first and then decide where all of the equipment should go. Taking two stairs at a time, Farid quickly ascends to the first floor. He pushes open the heavy office doors and enters, his steps slowing in astonishment at how much this space has changed.

Several blue and red electricity generators are stacked in the hallway. He also spots multiple Starlink antennas. The satellite internet constellation is run by SpaceX, the American aerospace manufacturer owned by Elon

Musk. Quirkily nicknamed 'Dishy McFlatface' by SpaceX, the antennas are sophisticated devices able to communicate with Starlink satellites in low Earth orbit and provide a stable internet connection from virtually anywhere in the world. The internet connection in Lviv is still reliable, but connectivity in the mountains of Ivano-Frankivsk, where we relocated part of the team, was challenging. The self-installable Starlink antenna was the perfect solution.

He makes his way down the hallway towards the room where he used to work. The office is barely recognisable, but the familiarity of the building's bones remains—the dent in the wall from where he lost his balance after a particularly enthusiastic *horilka* tasting, the spot on the colourful carpet where they had gathered to celebrate a milestone for the company, and the smell of old coffee that seems to linger in the corners despite the chaos of the current situation.

He is interrupted by Iurii's voice from the doorway.

'Farid! How are you?' he exclaims.

'Good to see you, Iurii,' Farid replies. 'The office has changed quite a bit. You've been busy. I brought everything you asked for. Where shall we put it?'

'We have turned the big storage room into a sort of equipment centre. Everything can go there. The office is a good base. It stood firm during the first attacks. The thick walls are paying off,' he laughs. 'I'll come down with you to help unload. Thanks for bringing it.'

They navigate their way back to the front door and out to Farid's Audi. As they descend the staircase, Iurii shares his experience from the month Farid spent in Poland and Germany. The assault on Lviv on 24 February initially remained an isolated incident. The subsequent days were marked by a major exodus in the east of Ukraine, with thousands of people transferring through Lviv on their way to the border.

'People grappled with the decision to either stay in Lviv, relocate to rural areas on the city's outskirts, or to leave Ukraine entirely,' Iurii recounts. 'Some of my friends contemplated whether to take to arms and move eastward to defend our homeland. Others took action by joining territorial defence forces for Lviv's region.'

'That's a tough decision. What made you decide to volunteer?' Farid asks.

'It didn't require much pondering. I love my country. I'm proud of Ukraine. I will never hesitate to die to defend it. I know of people who found loopholes to evade military service, but I didn't. I vowed to fight for Ukraine if the need arose, and now the time has come.'

For Iurii, the days since 24 February became a whirlwind of activity as he scrambled to understand where assistance was needed, how the military was organising volunteers, and what essential equipment he needed to get started immediately.

'I know that survival on the front line hinges on a stroke of luck,' he continued. 'Training, practice, and experience will tilt the odds in my favour, but there are aspects of an all-out war that I simply cannot control—random mines, enemy shells, friendly fire, and ricochets. It's best to come to terms with this stark reality before I find myself in the trenches.'

Opening the car's trunk, Farid cannot help but wince at the mountain of supplies he has managed to accumulate. Iurii eyes them with a grave kind of gratitude. They set to work, each picking up as many items as they can carry, their arms straining under the weight of the military vests, helmets, and bags filled with medical supplies. Their grunts of exertion break the heavy silence that has settled in the early evening. After multiple back-and-forths, they finally transfer the last supplies to the storage room. Farid slumps against the wall, taking a moment to catch his breath. He feels a sense of satisfaction, mixed with heavy sadness at the thought of what is to come. Iurii wipes the sweat off his forehead and turns to Farid, his gaze heavy but appreciative.

'How long will you be staying in Lviv?' he asks.

'Undecided. I'll see how things develop,' Farid replies.

'Okay. We had another attack last week, the first one since 24 February. Several missiles launched from warplanes over the Black Sea hit an aircraft repair plant, but there were no casualties. Let's go find the others now. They'll be glad to see you.'

Farid marks his return with a few rounds of *horilka* with the team, a welcome distraction from the nagging thought that he might not see them again for a long time. He returns home just before 11pm. A curfew has been introduced from midnight to 5am, turning the city into a ghost town at night.

Arriving at his apartment, Farid feels a twinge of unease as he turns the key in the lock. A shudder travels down his spine as he tries to recall the state in which he left it. Switching on the lights, he is greeted by the sight of clothes he had hastily left on the floor that pivotal Thursday. The forgotten fruit in the kitchen has rotted, spreading a sour odour in the apartment. The air feels heavy and stale, and he flings open the windows to let in some fresh air. After checking the contents of the fridge, he throws out most of the food that has exceeded its due date in the past month.

A walk across the city centre the next morning makes him realise how much the city he left a month ago has changed. The hotels, restaurants, and cafes are still crowded but now seem to host Ukrainians from the eastern parts of the country, relief workers, diplomats, and journalists rather than tourists. Most of the limestone statues in the city squares have been wrapped in foam and plastic for protection, turning their beautiful figures into unrecognisable silhouettes. Efforts are underway to safeguard the stained glass windows of the Basilica near the office by covering them with metal. Lviv's Palace of the Arts is bustling, with people packing jars of pickled preserves and organising mountains of donated clothes and trash bags filled with toiletries. Some stores are closed, and the street musicians he loved to watch on his walk back from the office have disappeared. Lviv feels overstuffed with emotion–energy and despair are palpable, mixed with anger and growing determination.

Farid grapples with the profound adjustment required to live in a war zone, where the sound of shelling alarms becomes a routine part of daily life. Predictable yet jarring, they rouse him from sleep in the early hours of the morning, forcing him to hurriedly make his way to the safety of the basement clad only in his pyjamas. The alarms often occur mid-conversation during work calls with his team in Germany, necessitating a hasty excuse as he rushes to join his neighbours in the basement. In the initial days, Farid finds himself lingering long after the alarm has ceased, waiting for his trembling body to regain a semblance of calm. Despite his mind gradually adapting to the relentless onslaught of terror, his body's primal survival instincts remain acutely responsive. Each alarm sends shock waves through his entire body, saturating every cell with a potent mix of fear and adrenaline. As he descends the stairs, his sweat-slicked hands falteringly seek support along the hallway walls, his unsteady legs struggling to bear his weight.

On his fifth day back in Lviv, as the alarms sound, he does not sprint to the basement as he has done countless times before. Instead, he finds himself standing at the stove, the aroma of sautéed vegetables filling the air, as he adds spices and stirs the pan with a newfound determination. For the first time, a sense of defiance surges within him, overpowering the instinct to flee. He is weary of the relentless running, exhausted by the vulnerability that permeates his days, and frustrated at feeling like a pawn in Russia's destructive game. As the air raid sirens continue their haunting melody, Farid, in a quiet act of resistance, turns up the volume on his iPad, immersing himself in the voices of a Netflix show he has been following while cooking. He sends a silent message of support to his friends. There were simply too many alarms to check in after each one. Instead, they have established a daily ritual of texting to inform each other that they are unharmed.

As Farid's initial week back in Lviv draws to a close, he finds himself slowly acclimatising to the constant presence of air raid sirens, their once petrifying howls gradually morphing into a source of irritation for disrupting his work calls, fragmenting his concentration, and jolting him from his sleep. Like the resilient Ukrainians around him, he strives to carve out a semblance of normality amidst the tumult of war. Yet no matter how steadfast his attempts to establish stability, whenever he feels somewhat grounded, a grim event shakes him again. This hits close to home this Wednesday, when Lesya, a dear friend, faces a near-death experience. While she is out for her penultimate driving lesson outside the city, a rocket plummets from the sky, landing a few hundred metres from the road. The impact sends earth and dirt spiralling into the air, blocking her vision with debris. Lesya slams the brakes, the force of the sudden stop propelling both her and her instructor forward, leaving them inches from the windshield. Miraculously, they emerge physically unharmed, albeit in shock. Terrifying and unexpected incidents like these continue to anchor Lviv's citizens to the harsh reality of the war, reminding them that despite their best efforts to continue with life as usual, they are living on borrowed time.

Farid finds himself at a crossroads, wrestling with the profound decision of whether to enlist in the army. In February, he returned to Lviv determined to defend the nation he has come to consider his home. Yet the more serious consideration he gives it, the more apparent the stark realities of the frontline become, along with the repercussions for both himself and his family. His Telegram channels are bombarding him with harrowing images and stories: mothers mourning their children, siblings tortured by the severed communication with their sisters at the frontline. In a matter that transcends life and death, Farid is facing the most formidable choice of his life.

A week later, on 18 April, he is jolted awake by explosions of a magnitude he has never experienced before. It is Monday, the start of the holy week leading up to Orthodox Easter Sunday, a time that, under different circumstances, would be marked by reflection and celebration. In the dark hours of the night, Russian forces have unleashed a barrage of attacks, striking more than 300 targets throughout Ukraine. Five missiles rain down upon Lviv. Failing to hit their target, the railway tracks that Farid has always regarded with a sense of foreboding on his journeys to the city, they ravage a military warehouse and a commercial service station where local drivers go for tyre repairs and car washes, transforming it into a chaotic scene. The attacks leave eleven people wounded and claim the lives of seven, marking the first reported casualties within the city limits since Russia's invasion of Ukraine on 24 February.

In the hotel next to the service station, the blast's force is powerful enough to blow out the windows. Broken glass and twisted metal turn into perilous obstacles for the residents who are roused abruptly from their slumber and are now running for their lives. Part of the roof of the two-storey building has been completely torn away, while smaller structures nearby bear the scars of significant damage. While the railroad tracks nearby were not damaged, they are littered with debris and scattered documents.

A mere 3.5 kilometres further southeast, Farid jumps out of his bed as the ground beneath him shakes violently. Rushing to the window, he is greeted by the sight of a towering column of smoke, visible even from fifteen kilometres away. The acrid smell of burning rubber pervades the air as he opens the window. Frantic voices in the stairway make it clear that his neighbours are taking the incident seriously.

'Run to the basement. Quick, run!' a neighbour's urgent command cuts through the air.

Farid hastily puts on his trousers and grabs a pullover, heeding the call that, while not explicitly directed at him, leaves no room for hesitation. In the basement, a heavy silence envelops the group as they sit huddled like they have not done since February. They trade Telegram messages, seeking updates and information about the blasts. The events of this morning have punctured the bubble of the normal life they strived so hard to maintain. The underground bunkers, often sparsely populated even during air raid sirens in recent times, are now filled to capacity.

Hours later, with the sirens quiet and the missiles stopped, news of the attacks reaches Farid's family and friends outside Ukraine. Their messages, laden with worry and concern, flood in. And while it is difficult for them to truly grasp the realities of his daily life, Farid finds himself in rare agreement on one unsettling truth: today, there is no safe place in Ukraine.

The following day, with the echoes of the blasts still resonating in his mind, he returns home.

View from Farid's apartment in Lviv, April 2022

BOYARKA

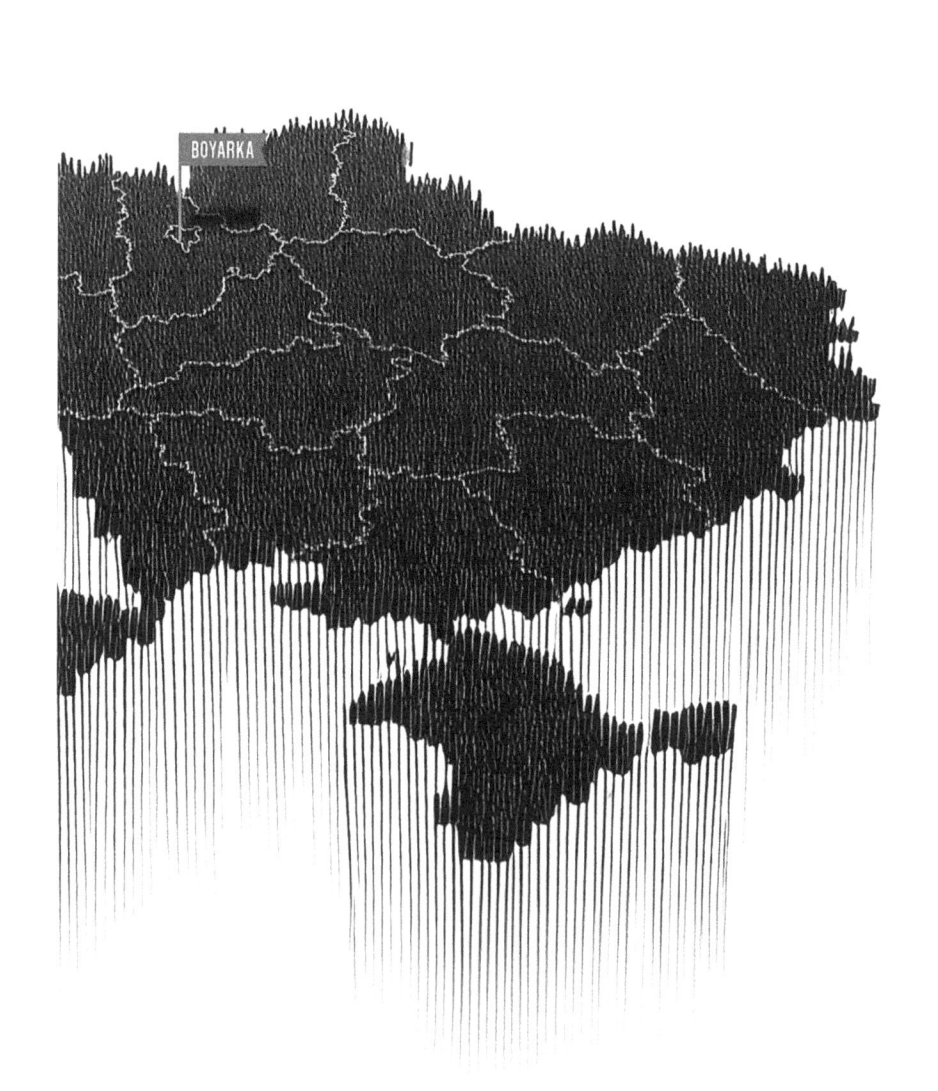

Chapter 18

A race against time

2 March 2022

It is Wednesday. We have been on the call for six days and six nights straight, and the learning curve remains steep, particularly for Larissa and me. By now, we are familiar with the names of most towns located near the Ukrainian border, and can more adeptly navigate the nuances in Ukrainian, Polish, and Russian spellings. Although our pronunciation remains incomprehensible to Danylo and Olena, we revel in every minor achievement. While brewing a fresh cup of tea in the kitchen, I continually repeat specific words out loud for practice. 'Проживання. *Prozyhyvannya. Prooozyyyyhyyyvannyyya.*'

We have lists of bomb shelters in various cities and are starting to grasp the layouts of towns we have never been to in person. We use Google Maps, Google Street View, and our Telegram channels to understand distances between places, identify routes through cities, and pinpoint areas considered particularly dangerous at the moment.

In the daily messages with our employees in Ukraine, we check in on their well-being—physical, mental, and financial. Shortly after Russia initiated its invasion, access to accounts in Ukraine's banking system was restricted. In a complex endeavour that puts our project management skills to the test, we provide each employee with a choice regarding their remuneration. They can opt to receive their wages through their Ukrainian bank accounts as usual, be paid into an international account, reroute the payment to a relative outside Ukraine, or, for those within our reach, receive payment in cash.

Based on the list we maintain on Notion, tracking names, locations, and urgent needs, we are now supporting well over two hundred people. While the situation continues to be dire and to change rapidly, today, for the first time, I feel as if we are beginning to get a handle on it. We have established a support structure that we can cling to amidst the chaos.

For the past week, I have felt almost isolated from the business outside our Google Meet call bubble. Our CEO, on the other hand, serves as our bridge to clients, suppliers, and supporters. He provides them with regular updates about our employees and the company. Many are interested because they care about the individuals whom they worked with as part of our shared projects. But for some, the connection to Ukraine is more personal. They have family or friends there, know someone in their close circles who does, or even have employees of their own in Ukraine. As the leader of the company, our CEO continues to keep them informed, and word of our support initiatives is spreading. Many wish they could offer similar assistance to those they care about.

Overnight, he receives a plea for help. In his characteristic haste, he offloads the task onto Larissa through a brief phone call. I am in the kitchen, carefully frothing the milk for my first cup of coffee of the day when I hear her voice ring out from the call.

'Stef, are you there?'

'I sure am,' I respond, after unmuting my microphone, the cup warming my cold hands. 'How are you doing?'

She takes a deep sigh. 'I'm not entirely sure. I just received a new request, and it's a bit overwhelming. Can we discuss how we might handle this?'

She then tells me the story of the person we have been asked to help, and a chill runs down my spine. Iryna is a fifty-four-year-old woman from

Boyarka, a small town just outside of Kyiv. She is the sister of one of our clients and works as a public servant, leading a simple yet fulfilling life in her hometown. A single woman with no children, she cherishes spending time with her close-knit group of girlfriends, taking invigorating bike rides through the town's verdant suburbs, and boasting of making the world's best Borscht. Her upright posture and steady hands radiate strength, while her muscular build leaves no doubt about her physical fitness.

However, Iryna's world was turned upside down barely a week ago when she was diagnosed with stage two brain cancer. For months, she had sensed that something was amiss, but had continually delayed her doctor's appointment, dismissing her morning headaches as a likely side effect of impending menopause. The headaches became relentless, and her usual painkillers provided less and less relief against the throbbing pain. Then came the sudden bouts of blurred vision, often striking while she was looking at the screen of her work computer. The accompanying nausea and dizziness were difficult to ignore. After her optometrist ruled out any decline in her vision, and after she had two fainting spells at work within a week, her best friend finally convinced her to seek a comprehensive medical examination.

Following a battery of tests, she found herself seated across from her doctor. His demeanour was calm and his gaze steady as he delivered the results of her scans. In a soothing and unwavering voice, he explained that they had discovered a stage two brain tumour. The five-year survival rate was 80% if they proceeded with immediate surgery; without it, she would be left with no more than twelve to fifteen months to live. The doctor's words that followed faded into a distant hum, as Iryna's mind was trapped in the moment, grappling with the devastating news she had just received.

Her life-saving surgery was scheduled at Kyiv Regional Clinical Hospital for Saturday, 26 February 2022. However, on that fateful morning, the battle for control of Ukraine's capital was in full swing, the dissonant echoes of gunfire reverberating through the city as Russian troops advanced.

When it became clear that all surgeries would have to be postponed, Iryna and her brother found themselves embroiled in a heated discussion on the phone. She remained hopeful that the situation would normalise soon and that she would be able to receive the necessary treatment locally. Her brother firmly believed that her best chance was to leave Ukraine immediately and seek treatment elsewhere. As in their childhood disagreements, her elder brother had the final word.

'She will board a train bound for Poland tomorrow, and transfer to Germany from there,' Larissa informs me. 'She'll arrive tomorrow night and they are clueless about how to arrange the urgent brain surgery she desperately needs. Both travel and local insurance will refuse to cover it because it's a preexisting condition.'

Thus, for the coming hours, we find ourselves thrust into a research frenzy, battling against not just the timeline of her impending arrival but the relentless ticking of the clock against her life-saving surgery. Larissa and I try to stay calm while searching for health insurance plans that cover pre-existing conditions without waiting periods, and specialists willing to perform emergency surgeries pro bono. The hours roll by as we navigate a sea of bureaucracy and medical jargon.

The magnitude of the responsibility we have accepted only dawns on me later. Amidst his despair, our client is in search of a solution. He carries the burden of an older brother, feeling an overwhelming need to save his sister, yet the gravity of the situation leaves him nearly paralysed. It is a cruel twist of fate that Iryna's life hangs in the balance simply because her scheduled surgery collided with Russia's invasion.

In our earnest desire to help, and the determination to confront any challenge thrown our way, we assumed responsibilities that were not ours to bear, and we felt the immense pressure that came with them. Moving a workforce out of a war zone was one thing, but orchestrating the evacuation of a cancer patient in desperate need of life-saving surgery was an entirely different matter. For Larissa, this pressure surfaces as waves of anxiety and a profound sense of responsibility, while stirring a turbulent tide of confidence and fear about our capacity to handle the situation in me.

After numerous dead-ends, we finally find an insurer willing to cover the surgery as well as the subsequent post-surgical care and medication, and a hospital to operate.

Our CEO shares what we discovered with Iryna's brother, and we hold our breaths collectively till we hear back from him. At last, we receive a text message. By a stroke of serendipity, coupled with the relentless efforts of her doctors, Iryna will be able to receive her operation in a hospital located a few hundred kilometres from Kyiv.

Several weeks later, we receive a call from Iryna's brother. His voice, strained with gratitude and relief, conveys further good news—Iryna's surgery was a success. She is on the road to recovery, and there is a significant chance that she will be able to lead a normal life once more. It is a minor victory in the vast context of the war, but one that serves as a powerful reminder. In the darkest of times, these small triumphs are beacons of hope, and reignite our determination to keep going.

KHARKIV

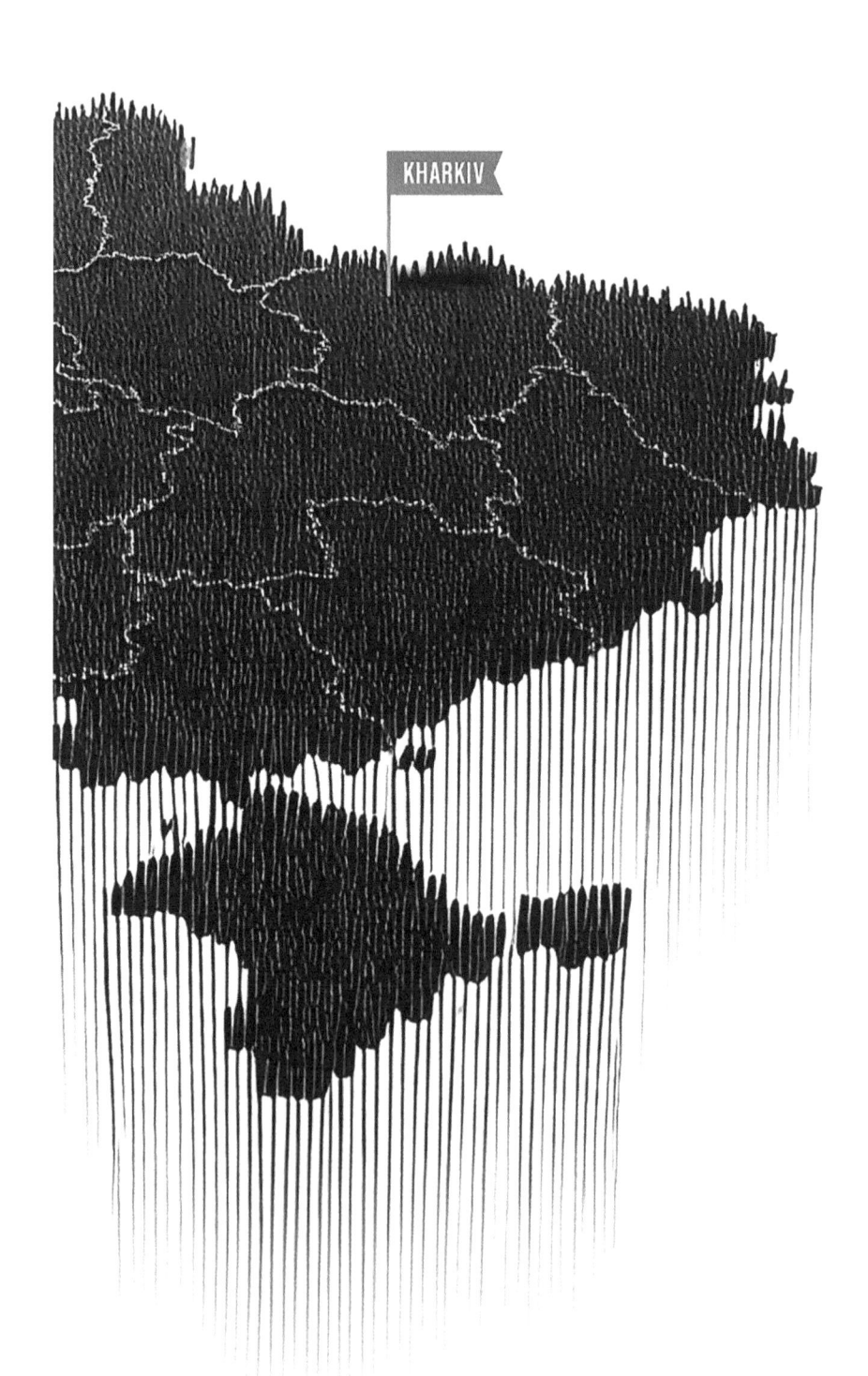

Chapter 19

My home, near the front line

2 March 2022

In the afternoon of Wednesday, our relentless efforts to establish a safe shelter in western Ukraine finally come to fruition. Today marks the beginning of our accommodation bookings in Polyanitsya, and in a matter of days, the first families will start to arrive.

Among them is Natalia's family: her husband Ivan, and their two sons, who are twelve and fourteen years old. Just forty-eight hours prior, they had left the bomb shelter in Kharkiv that had been their refuge for an agonising six days.

Kharkiv is Ukraine's second-largest city, after the capital Kyiv, and is located a mere forty kilometres from the Russian border. It's a city of contrasts, where historic lanes intersect with contemporary boulevards and centuries-old traditions intertwine with the hustle and bustle of a modern metropolis. As one of Ukraine's cultural hubs, it houses a plethora of theatres, museums, and galleries. Often dubbed the 'city of students', Kharkiv also prides itself on its numerous higher education institutions. Its geographical proximity to Russia has had an undeniable impact on the city throughout history. Many residents of the city and its surrounding regions are bilingual, speaking both Ukrainian and Russian. As a crossroads of the two cultures, it is a rich tapestry of traditions, literature, and arts from both nations. Generations of migration between Kharkiv and Russian cities have woven a network of familial ties, often bridging the two nationalities.

Natalia's family resided in an apartment on the topmost floor of a modern building in Kharkiv's southern neighbourhood called Osnovyanskyi. In the early hours of 24 February 2022, an alarming noise jolted her awake. Within minutes, the piercing screams of neighbours echoed through the building. Dashing down the hallway towards her sons' bedrooms, she was met halfway by her older son, panic evident in his eyes.

'Mum, what's happening?' his voice trembled.

'I'm not sure yet. Quick, go to the bathroom and stay away from the windows,' she urged.

She darted into her second son's room. He was a tight sleeper and was still too groggy to move in a coordinated fashion. Grasping him firmly, she pulled him towards her, and held tight to his arm as she guided him down the corridor to the bathroom.

Meanwhile, Ivan gauged the proximity of the explosions peering through the window. His sturdy fingers began typing frantic texts to friends further north-east who reported fierce fighting between Ukrainian and Russian troops. He swiftly sealed all the windows with sturdy tape in a crosshatch pattern and drew the curtains shut. Taking a quick look around the rooms, he moved obvious flammable and loose items to safe places before joining his family in the bathroom.

Crouching on the cold tile floor, they tried to make sense of the chaos unfolding outside. Their cat Rubik huddled with them, trembling with fear of the air raid siren's eerie, relentless wail. Still in shock themselves, Natalia and Ivan deliberated their next move. They had considered this scenario but dismissed it, struggling to believe that Putin would actually act on his threats.

Taking a breath, Ivan made the decisive call.

'The apartment is no longer safe. Our building's height makes us an easy mark for aerial strikes, and we're particularly vulnerable on the top floor. We need to head underground right away.'

In mere moments, they gathered their essentials into a bag. Casting a final, sorrowful glance at Rubik, and hoping that he would be safe, they closed the door behind them. With their hastily packed belongings in tow, they sped down the stairwell, out of the building, and toward the throngs of people heading towards the closest basements, metro stations, and bomb shelters a short distance away. It was still pitch black, and a frosty wind cut through the −5 degree Celsius chill, seeping mercilessly through the layers of their clothing. The nerve-racking wail of the air raid sirens, which seemed to grow louder by the minute, jolted away any remnants of sleep from this night that had so abruptly come to an end.

Their steps illuminated by the muted glow of streetlights, they hastened along the sidewalks as quickly as their legs and the dense crowd permitted. It would not be long till the same streets would be covered with shards of glass, the skeletal remains of buildings, and pieces of facades. With every heartbeat, as they pressed on, the Russians were narrowing the gap, clashing vehemently with Ukraine's artillery—a defence that would, by day's end, succeed in halting their advance further southward.

Within fifteen minutes, they reached an old five-storey apartment building which they knew had a basement. It was brimming with people and their hastily-packed possessions. Every conceivable space was claimed, leaving only a narrow path to its entrance. The vast room's stark white walls contrasted with green pipes running horizontally above them. A haphazard assortment of wooden, plastic, and fabric armchairs, showing their age, lined the walls. Quickly taking a small claim to space, the family settled in, securing the last two chairs for the children while Natalia and Ivan placed themselves on cardboard laid on the ground.

Though the air was only marginally warmer than outside, the basement provided a respite from the wind's bite. The air lacked oxygen and smelled of musty blankets, dank urban chill, and damp clothing. Tension and worry hung in the air, and as Natalia's crystal-blue eyes scanned the room, she could see the sorrow in others' eyes. There were people of all ages and from all walks of life: elderly people, many of them seemingly alone; young families with toddlers; mothers cradling infants; young couples; and pet owners clutching their feline companions to their chests, seeking and offering comfort in equal measure.

Finally able to take a breath, Ivan reached out to Bogdan, his son-in-law and one of our company's technical leads located in Germany, to update him on the evolving situation.

'Bogdan, it's happening. We're in the bomb shelter down the road near the cemetery, trying to determine our next steps. What do you want us to do with your cat Rubik?'

Bogdan replied swiftly. 'I'm so sorry. How can we help? Just leave Rubik at your apartment. Your safety is paramount.'

As dawn hit the horizon, Ivan dared to step outside to witness a sky blanketed in smoke, the aftermath of bombs detonating across Kharkiv, launched from across the border in Belgorod just moments earlier. When the air raid sirens finally fell silent, he rushed back to the apartment and collected blankets, pillows and camping mattresses to create makeshift beds. Until they had an exit plan, they needed to make their shelter as habitable as possible. That same day, Kharkiv's city council imposed a curfew spanning from 10pm to 6am, urging residents to remain indoors during these times.

Life in the basement settled into a monotonous rhythm. There wasn't much to do except wait, and the family sought distractions where they could. Once a day, Ivan returned to the apartment to feed Rubik and gather food.

Mornings saw brief outdoor excursions with the boys for a breath of fresh air. All too often, their hands were still shaking with the panic caused by the blood-curdling sound of explosions during the night. The duet of Ukrainian artillery and Russian missiles punctuated every hour of the night. By Friday, intense combat had ignited in Kharkiv's northern districts. Ukrainian forces fortified their positions, notably around the village of Tsyrkuny just outside the city. Come Saturday, the curfew's commencement was brought forward to 6pm. Russian troops were mounting incursions into the city from multiple flanks, including the west, where they were halted only at the Pisochyn suburb. On Monday, rocket strikes killed and wounded dozens of civilians. Russian forces destroyed electrical substations in the city, disconnecting several districts in Kharkiv from power, heat, and water. Life in the city became increasingly unbearable.

Some of the young men sleeping on the far end of the vast hall began to bring *horilka* from their brief daytime outings from the shelter.

'It's the only way I can sleep,' one of them remarked, noticing the disapproving glance from a woman beside him.

As the days drifted by, Natalia observed the elderly man next to her increasingly engrossed in photos on his phone. In those snapshots, he appeared cheerful and elegant, bearing little resemblance to the man she now sat next to, his skin pallid. He had been wearing the same dirty tracksuit since his arrival four days prior. She recognised him as a fellow resident from their vast apartment building, having exchanged casual greetings with him in the stairwell. Beyond those fleeting encounters, they knew little about one another. Now they lived together in this makeshift refuge, devoid of any barriers and personal space. Their hasty departure from the apartment on Thursday morning had stripped away all semblance of privacy.

With the shelter's grim reality becoming increasingly oppressive, murmurs about whether to stay or evacuate began circulating.

'I don't have the means to live elsewhere, and I don't know what I'd do if I left. But if I stay here, I might die,' lamented an elderly woman who sought refuge in the bomb shelter after Russian missiles destroyed her home in the city's south on Friday.

A young mother nodded in agreement. 'I'm uncertain if anywhere in Ukraine is safer at this moment. At least this is our city, our home.'

By Tuesday, respite seemed even more distant. The wail of the air raid sirens reliably marked the transition from day to night, and from night to day. Missiles pierced the silence of the night, rendering the makeshift stool-and-cardboard-beds intolerable. Though Natalia's sons were resilient, the shelter's oppressive circumstances and sheer exhaustion were starting to take a visible toll on them. The frequency of the explosions, sometimes multiple times an hour, made it impossible to imagine how anyone could live in Kharkiv for much longer.

'If we stay, we'll be condemned to life underground. I don't want our family to endure this any longer,' Ivan whispered to Natalia. 'Tomorrow, we'll leave, too.'

Chapter 20

A journey into the unknown

2 March 2022

On Wednesday morning, at 6am, the end of the daily curfew, Ivan returns to the apartment to pick up Rubik while the family prepares to leave the shelter. Reaching the central station to catch the train westward is a challenge. All public transport has come to a standstill. Metro stations and tunnels have been repurposed as bomb shelters, housing thousands of Kharkiv's residents, who were trying to escape the relentless Russian bombardment. Leaving the bomb shelter means running the gauntlet, with the ever-present danger of becoming a victim of one of the many missiles Russia mercilessly drops on Kharkiv every day.

They are not the only ones who have decided that the risk of leaving is better than the chance of facing the advancing Russian soldiers from the front line in Kharkiv while they are trapped in the bomb shelter. A neighbour has also decided to embark on an escape today.

'I'm 69, so martial law doesn't apply to me. I'll cross into Poland to join my daughter. Once the curfew lifts on Wednesday morning, I can give you a lift to the train station,' he said to Ivan last night.

7am marks the time of their departure. The typically short car ride from their district to the central station is nerve-racking. But for once, the air raid alarms remain silent.

Kharkiv-Passenger, the city's central station, is one of the major railway hubs in Ukraine. The imposing yellow structure, crowned by its forty-two-metre high towers, serves as a gateway for both domestic and international train travel. The vast square in front of the station is a hive of activity. Hundreds are trying to push through the large black swing doors leading to the concourse area and the platforms. Amidst the throng, it is hard to navigate and stay together.

'Hold on to my jacket,' Natalia instructs the children, while Ivan uses his arms to forge a path through the dense crowd.

Their bags and Rubik's cat carrier repeatedly get caught between people's legs, compelling them to lean in with all their weight just to keep moving. The train announcement boards display the schedule for evacuation trains heading west and make a plea for kindness and understanding in these dire times.

The ticket hall is a whirlwind of movement. Some people seek respite on the floor, attempting to catch a few moments of sleep amidst the chaos, while the majority jostle towards the ticket counters, seeking passage even though tickets are scarce. The floor has all but vanished beneath a mosaic of jackets, bags, pet carriers, and anxious faces that take up every square centimetre. Trains are operating on a first come, first served basis, and boarding is challenging even with a ticket in hand. For those desperate to escape, there are two types of tickets: the coveted free passes for the evacuation trains, which are almost mythical in their scarcity, and regular service tickets, which are sold out until well into March. It is evident that some have camped at the station for days, waiting to get a spot on any westward-bound train, the only somewhat safe direction to go from Kharkiv.

The stairways leading to the platforms are equally congested, with people standing seven rows deep. The packed crowd leaves scant room even to stand, much less manoeuvre. The brothers crouch down, hugging their knees, to get some rest while they comfort Rubik. Time seems to crawl as everyone waits for the next train to pull into the station. When it finally arrives, the mass of people begins to move. The family finds itself immersed in a human tide, inching towards the platforms as the first people board the train. But after a few metres, they come to a halt yet again. The train is packed, leaving them to wait for the next one.

'Mum, I'm exhausted,' one of the brothers murmurs. 'When will it be our turn?'

'I wish I knew, dear. Unfortunately, it seems like we might have to wait a little longer,' Natalia replies softly, sharing a concerned look with Ivan.

After an agonising eight-hour wait, Ivan, Natalia, and their sons squeeze onto a train bound westward. They are not sure where exactly it is going, but its direction offers a glimmer of hope. Compartments designed as sleeper berths are now crammed with ten or more passengers. Benches meant for two now seat three, and many, like Ivan's family, have to face the long journey standing in the corridors. The conductor's announcement that the train is at capacity is met with pleas of desperation. Still, more passengers jam their way in as the doors close and the train starts to move. It leaves behind dejected faces as it rolls out of the station. Abandoned bags and a shattered pram on the tracks are a testament to the chaos.

The air within the train carriage is suffocating, and the atmosphere palpably tense. Several hours into their journey, they receive a message from Bogdan. Full of concern, he asks about their whereabouts and destination. Yet neither Ivan nor Natalia can answer either question. From their position, with the view obstructed by other passengers, all they can tell him for the moment is that a city is zipping past them.

Seven hours later, the train comes to an abrupt halt as they reach their final destination, Kyiv. Passengers hoping to continue west towards Lviv will need to transfer. The family disembarks one by one, unsure where to go. Other passengers seem to feel the weight of uncertainty as well. Where to next? An elderly woman in a blue-patterned headscarf is helped off the train by a young man and slowly walks away in silence. Nearby, a young mother clutches her child as she stands motionless among her bags, appearing lost amidst the sea of people.

The cacophony of thousands at the station is occasionally pierced by chilling sirens and distant explosions indicating imminent air raids. Kyiv's train station is a mirror image of Kharkiv's—teeming with refugees, all searching for a passage westward to safety. Tragically, less than four hours ago, a devastating explosion from a downed Russian cruise missile shook the very foundations of this station, where thousands of men, women, and children are evacuating.

Four hours later, they board their second train destined for Lviv. Bogdan hoped the family would reach Przemyśl, the first station in Poland just beyond the border. To ease their journey, he reached out to a local contact for support to find temporary accommodation where the family could rest. However, as the day wore on, it became evident that they would not make it this far and yet had to face the painful decision of potentially leaving Ivan behind due to martial law restrictions. So Bogdan left a message on our company's Telegram channel asking for help. Danylo and Yurii responded immediately. Danylo quickly arranged for two rooms at our accommodation in Polyanitsya, and Yurii generously offered to pick the family up from the Lviv train station and host them at his home until they could gather the strength for the next leg of their journey.

In the early hours of Thursday, the train finally enters Lviv station. The sky is a grim shade of winter grey. Faces etched with fatigue and worry peer out from the windows, with passengers having endured hours of cramped conditions, rampant uncertainty, and the heartache of leaving their homes behind.

Yurii stands in the station's parking lot, holding a sign with Ivan's family name. He has seen a photo shared on Telegram which he is using as a reference, having never met the family in person. He adjusts his glasses and takes a deep breath, his eyes scanning the tide of passengers exiting the building.

Suddenly, he spots them: a couple with two young boys, clearly weary, with clothes rumpled from the long journey, clutching big bags and a cat carrier. As they look around, their expressions waver between relief and apprehension. Yurii approaches them with a reassuring smile, extending a welcoming hand to Ivan.

'You must be Ivan,' he greets Ivan warmly. 'I'm Yurii. It's a relief to see that you have made it to Lviv safely.'

Ivan meets Yurii's gaze, his eyes filled with gratitude. 'Yes, that's me. Thank you for coming,' he responds, his voice strained from fatigue.

'Let's get you home. Your family needs rest.'

The unfamiliarity of relying on the benevolence of strangers is disconcerting, but Yurii's generosity is heartwarming. They had never moved in with another family, let alone one they had never met before. When they arrive at Yurii's home, his wife mirrors his hospitality. A hearty meal awaits them, and the guest room has been meticulously prepared. Overwhelmed by the arduous journey of the past day, they fall asleep the moment they settle into the beds in the guest room. The night is fleeting, seemingly ending as soon as it begins.

The next morning, Ivan and Natalia explore how the family could continue their journey to Polyanitysa and find someone online to give them a lift. The drive from Lviv to Polyanitsya, though little more than 230 kilometres, takes more than four hours. Narrow mountainous paths lead them through the pristine, snow-covered Carpathian forests.

Polyanitsya, renowned for its picturesque scenery, is a quaint mountain town lined with resorts that typically attract numerous ski enthusiasts during this season. However, Natalia, usually one to appreciate the beauty of nature, barely notices it. As the snow-draped landscapes speed past her, she is consumed by thoughts of the uncertain future her children are now facing. As parents, it is their responsibility to look after them. Perhaps they should have taken Russia's threats more seriously and left earlier. At the very least, they ought to have prepared an exit plan to avoid being left stranded like this with the boys in tow.

Now faced with a dilemma, the family is in limbo. Due to martial law, Ivan is trapped, and the thought of leaving him behind is unfathomable for Natalia. While the German company that both her daughter Anastasiia and her son-in-law Bogdan work for has graciously offered them this refuge in the mountains, it is merely a temporary solution. The boys need stability, some kind of normality, and perspective. Their education cannot be left hanging, and with each harrowing day spent in this war, Natalia fears that they might bear scars for the rest of their lives.

Yet, for a fleeting moment, there seems to be a return to normality. In the backseat, the brothers are animatedly debating some inconsequential detail. Overhearing them, one could almost think that a good night's sleep has erased the horrors of the past few days. But Natalia knows better.

Four and a half hours later, they reach their destination in Polyanitsya. The boys' eyes widen with wonder, and they press their noses eagerly against the windows as the car pulls into the driveway. The building in front of them is impressive—a quintessential ski chalet as is commonly seen here in Bukovel, Polyanitysa's most popular skiing area. Beyond its doors lies another unknown living situation far from home. With a mix of hope and fatigue, they take a deep breath and press down on the handle.

BUKOVEL

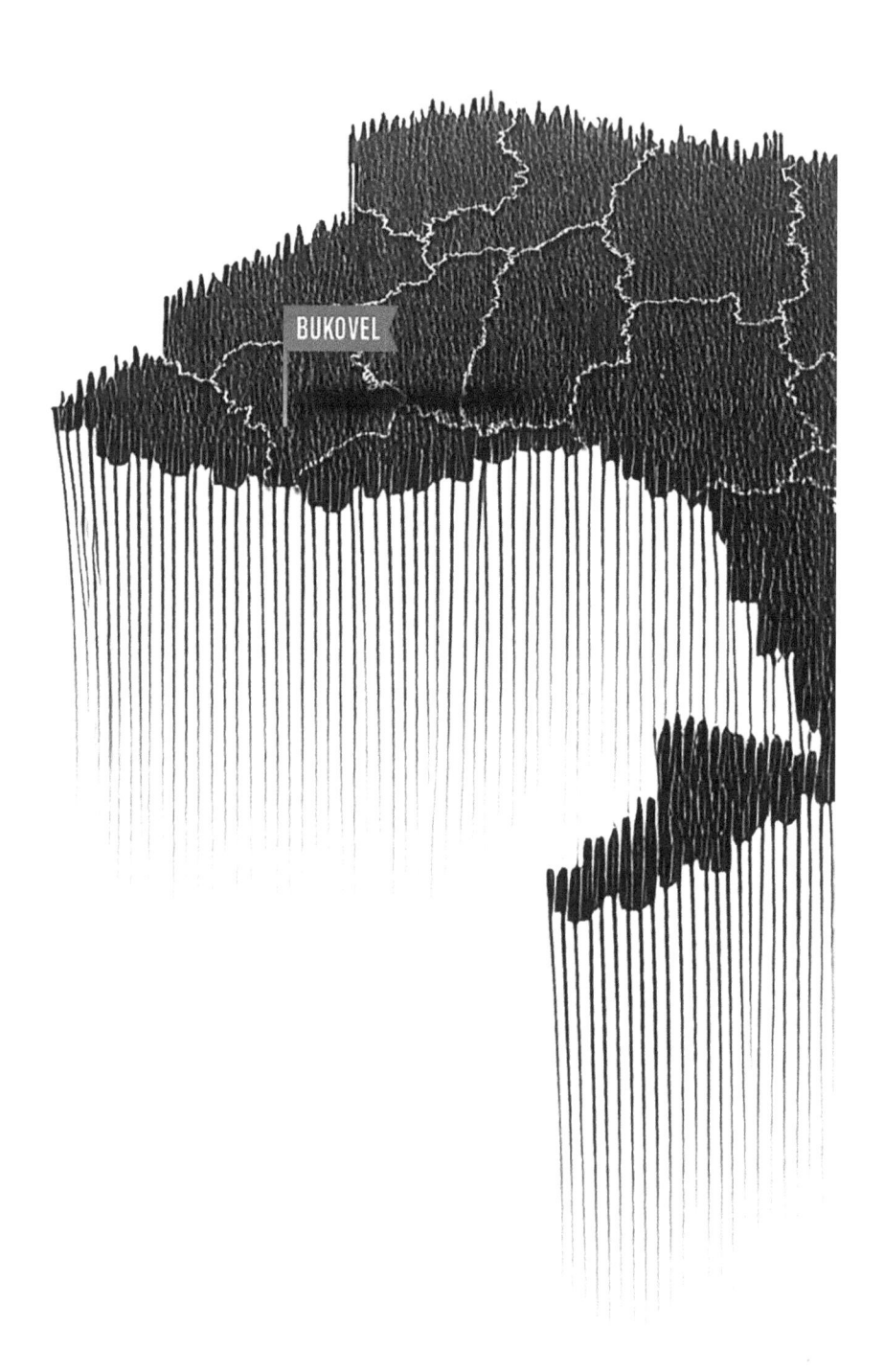

Chapter 21

Sheltered, yet adrift

4–27 March 2022

As the door in Bukovel resists, opening only centimetre by centimetre with soft jolts, Ivan pushes it in with more determination and opens it. It is a large house with two storeys. The door opens to a small hallway with several pairs of shoes neatly stacked on a little shoe rack to the right. From what Ivan can tell, at least three other adults have already arrived. A sturdy wooden door separates the entrance from the living area, and a dim light shines from underneath it. His family hustles in behind him, eager to escape the freezing temperatures outside.

He opens the second door. Things seem quiet inside. There is a generous living space. The floor, walls, and ceiling are lined with wood in a soft yellow hue. Two large lined woven carpets are on the floor, in between a dining set made from European Beech, a tree often found in the Carpathian mountains surrounding the house. The table is neatly set for three people, with side dishes already placed in the middle. On the other side of the carpets are a foosball table, a comfortable-looking sofa, and a small living room table with board games stacked under it. This side of the room also has a chimney, where a fire warms the room. Two cats are sleeping side by side on it, nestled close to each other and enjoying the warmth emanating from the flames. They barely lift their heads as the family enters. Softly opening an eye, they determine that the family is not to be worried about, and go straight back to sleep. The fire's crackling is the only sound to be heard on the lower floor of the house. The wall opposite the window is lined with three more doors. All of them are closed, there is no sign of the other inhabitants.

Just as the boys jolt towards the foosball table, they hear voices and a dog's bark coming from upstairs. Ivan turns to Natalia, sharing an assuring nod and walks towards the stairs leading up to the second floor.

'Boys, stop playing now. We don't know who this foosball table belongs to. Come up with us first and we'll work it out later,' Natalia tells her sons.

They reluctantly follow her up the stairs, which lead to a wide open space lined with a large bookshelf and a generous kitchen on the other side. As she hears the family come up, a friendly woman, standing at the stove, turns towards them and welcomes them with a smile.

'Hi. I'm Ludmila. My husband Petro, my daughter Lesya, and I arrived two days ago. You must be Ivan and Natalia. Danylo mentioned you were arriving today.'

Ivan and Natalia nod, shaking Ludmila's hand. For a brief moment, they stand there, taking in the situation. How much life has changed in the past few days. They had a home and a life. Now they are about to cohabitate with people they have never met—the family of their daughter's co-worker.

'You must be tired,' Ludmila continues. 'There are two free bedrooms on this floor. We sleep downstairs. There are two bathrooms on each floor. Only the kitchen and dining room are shared. Would you like to join us for dinner? It's almost ready.'

Only now does Ivan notice his stomach grumble in agreement. The drive and anxiety about what would await them in Bukovel have distracted the family for hours.

'Yes please, I'm so hungry,' one of their sons blurts out before Natalia can respond. She gives him a disciplining look. Then she turns back to Ludmila and returns the smile.

'We'd love to, thank you. I'll wash my hands and come help you.'

As they sit around the dinner table, the families begin to share their stories. Ludmilla, Petro, and Lesya hail from Mykolaiv, a city with a population of 500,000 in the southern part of Ukraine. Strategically positioned at the confluence of the Southern Bug and Ingul Rivers, and approximately sixty-five kilometres from the Black Sea coast, Mykolaiv is famous for its bridges that connect various sections of the city, facilitating transit across the Southern Bug, a vital waterway.

Renowned for her prudence and intuition, Ludmilla had urged her family to prepare for the worst as early as 21 February. They had stocked up on cash and non-perishable food, filled their gas tanks, and packed their emergency bags. When the full-scale invasion commenced on 24 February, the family evacuated to the countryside. They took their dog and four cats with them, hoping to find safety in the country house owned by Ludmilla's parents.

For the first five days, they woke each morning to the sound of missiles. While it was terrifying, they remained sixty kilometres from home, which was as far as they were prepared to venture then. Petro continued to commute to the city each day for work. His journey was fraught with risk, considering that he had to cross the Varvarivskyi bridge over the Southern Bug river, a likely target for Russian forces. He coordinated with a co-worker to start his shift early, allowing him to leave at 4pm instead of his usual 8pm and make it back to the house before the daily curfew. As he crossed the bridge on his return journey on 25 February, he was the very last to do so before it was closed by Ukrainian officials. Russian helicopters hovered above him, while all he could do was hold the steering wheel tightly and pray that he would make it to the other side and back to the country house alive. Yet he went back the next day. As an electrician, he was committed to addressing the power disruptions that had plagued Mykolaiv since the onset of Russia's attack. Highly committed to his job, he had not missed a day at work in almost twenty years.

Ludmilla had an equally deeply rooted connection to Mykolaiv, where she had been born, met her husband, and given birth to her child. Starting her career as a teacher in the very same neighbourhood that they had lived in for more than twenty years, Ludmilla climbed the ranks over the years and currently serves as a principal of a local school.

When Lesya, who works as a designer at our company, first informed her parents about the safe houses in Bukovel, they immediately dismissed the idea. Their devotion to their jobs and Mykolaiv was profound, making the thought of abandoning the life they loved so much unimaginable.

Then, on the sixth day, in the first hours of the morning, the village's air raid siren sounded unexpectedly. It did not take long for them to realise why. Peering out of the windows through the curtains, they spotted Russian troops marching through the countryside a mere fifty metres from their house. Lesya watched her mother freeze in fear. They hid and held their breaths until the soldiers passed. Although nothing further ensued, the sight of Russian troops was enough to change her parents' minds. The following day, the family began to plan their journey westward. They packed their things and left before breakfast the next morning, with all their pets in tow, embarking on a long drive in a cramped car. The journey spanned three days, marred by endless traffic jams and multiple stops at friends' homes due to the nightly curfew in place for most of the country.

Upon their arrival in Bukovel, the cats relished the chance to finally leave their crates. They eagerly explored their new environment, quickly finding favourite spots to curl up across the house's three storeys.

Two days in, they seem to adapt to their new surroundings far faster than their owners. Though Bukovel is picturesque, the family feels more isolated than ever before in their lives. Lesya finds solace and distraction in her work, reconnecting with her team online. For her parents, however, the adjustment is more challenging. Accustomed to jobs that require their physical presence, they find themselves out of work and spend their days engrossed in the news, meticulously tracing the military developments of the previous night each morning, and anticipating Russia's next moves. Keeping in touch with friends and family consumes a great deal of energy. They check on the safety of their friends and relatives daily, learning where the bombs have struck and whether their homes remain unscathed. Residing in the safe house in Bukovel offers as much relief as it does guilt—for having left while their loved ones remain in danger, for the brief moments of feeling safe when they are not, and for the forced farewells every day, laden with the uncertainty of whether their friends would survive the night, through which they sleep.

Days begin to blend into one another. The only breaks in the monotony are the brisk morning walks with the dog, the frosty air nipping at exposed skin, and trips to the only supermarket in Bukovel. While the notion of sharing a house with strangers initially caused some discomfort, as weeks slide into one another, both families grow increasingly thankful for each other's company. The kitchen, once just a functional room, becomes a space where Ludmila and Natalia exchange stories and connect. They find comfort in speaking with someone who fully grasps the gravity of the situation and shares the emotional toll it exacts—offering fleeting respite in this time of existential boredom. When they first left their homes, they expected to be away for only a few days, perhaps weeks at most. However, three weeks into their stay in Bukovel, the situation on the frontline only seems to worsen.

Petro, preferring solitude, spends hours by the window, his gaze distant and thoughtful. He replays the familiar clang of machinery and the banter of colleagues from his old life in Mykolaiv—a life punctuated by the satisfaction of solving tangible problems. His days, once marked by precise tasks and clear objectives, now melt into long hours filled with anxiety and restlessness. Though his lung disease exempts him from military service, he feels sidelined in a war in which he believes he should be fighting, at least by maintaining the power supply or repairing critical infrastructure, doing what he knows best.

One chilly afternoon, as Lesya lifts her eyes from her notebook, she notices her father outside, shovelling snow for the third time that day. His face, determined yet weary, catches the dull winter light. He pushes the heavy snow aside—a Sisyphean task given that it has been snowing all day and the paths will likely be covered again soon. Observing him, she realises how much she misses his once frequent mischievous laughter. Now, it comes sparingly and feels forced, as if he is trying to reassure not just his family but himself.

She puts on her coat and steps out, crossing her arms against the biting wind that sneaks under her clothes, sending shivers down her spine.

'Hi, Dad. How are you? You've been out here for a while. I'm a bit worried about your lungs,' she says, her voice laced with honest concern.

'I'm fine, Lesya. It's not me we should be worrying about. Most men are facing a much tougher fate these days defending our country,' he replies without pausing his labour.

She falls silent for a moment, watching him as he keeps shovelling, the sweat on his brow defying the freezing temperature. His activity barely masks the deeper turmoil. Her father, once a pillar of strength and constancy, now appears diminished, lacking every purpose in this new, idle environment.

'It's true,' she finally responds, stepping closer. 'But I can tell you're exhausted. Maybe take a break and come back out later?'

'No, I can't,' he blurts out, pausing this time to lean on his shovel. 'I can't just sit around all day any more. I was meant to do my part to protect our country and I can't. I was meant to do the job I've done for more than thirty years and instead, I'm stuck here, doing nothing. If I'm not useful to anyone, what am I doing here?' His voice is stern, his eyes meeting hers with an intensity that brooks no argument.

Regret flickers across his face as soon as the words leave his mouth. She cannot grasp the weight of the decisions that have been haunting him, nor can he find the words to explain. Day by day, the thoughts that maybe they should have stayed, that maybe he could have done more, plague him.

Lesya's heart aches with compassion and helplessness. Taking a deep breath, she turns back towards the house. She wants to help, to say or do something that would ease his pain, but any words feel trivial against the sheer scale of what he is experiencing.

What he was forced to leave behind is so much more than a job, and what he needs, she cannot provide—a new sense of purpose and belonging.

Bukovel, February 2022

Destroyed governmental building in the centre of Mykolayiv

Varvaryvsky Bridge

Chapter 22

Storms and bad omens

4 March 2022

In Germany, Anastasiia and Bogdan are relieved to know that the family is safe in the Carpathian mountains. A Ukrainian in his mid-twenties, Bogdan has jet-black hair cropped short and keen eyes that compliment his soft facial features. His gentle smile radiates a youthful vitality and a deep inner calm, making him effortlessly approachable to other people and a much-appreciated colleague in his new office.

He and Anastasiia both grew up in Kharkiv and share a background in Computer Science. After spending two years in Oslo, they landed in Germany merely one week ago. Bogdan worked for a Norwegian company which, after a year of his having worked remotely from Kharkiv, had offered to relocate him to Oslo. With most Norwegians speaking English fluently, life in the city was easy to navigate. They cherished their morning commutes alongside Oslo's harbour, savoured Lutefisk (a traditional Norwegian dish of dried whitefish, commonly enjoyed during Christmas time), and relished their weekend escapes to the fjords.

Yet, after eighteen months, both felt the itch for adventure again. Germany had long been on their bucket list. One of Bogdan's former colleagues from Ukraine now worked in western Germany and offered for him to join her team. Intrigued, he applied, and his initial impressions of the company during his interview were overwhelmingly positive. The company was growing fast and looking for individuals skilled in data and coding. Anastasiia interviewed as well and secured a position as a Data Engineer.

She is not one to command the room, yet illuminates it when she speaks. Her radiant reddish-brown hair cascades past her shoulders, and her green eyes, always observant, reflect her analytical mind. They gleam with kindness and a genuine interest in others, making her radiate humility and warmth.

When they decided to relocate to Germany, they took a few months off in between jobs to visit their families in Kharkiv. This reunion was overdue as the Covid-19 pandemic had made it impossible for them to travel to Ukraine. In December 2021, they touched down in eastern Ukraine, planning to embark for Germany by February 2022. On 11 February, after an enjoyable two-month stay with their families, Bogdan found himself checking flights from Kharkiv to Dortmund, a city in Germany's west. They compared prices and booked a flight for Thursday, 17 February 2022, not anticipating that this date would be a mere week before Russia's invasion.

In the weeks leading up to their departure, Anastasiia and Bogdan found themselves in a psychological tug-of-war. On the one hand, they were consumed by the exhilarating prospect of relocating to Germany, juggling logistical concerns from securing housing to preparing for their job onboarding, and ensuring the well-being of their cherished cat, Rubik. On the other hand, the mounting tension from Russia was impossible to ignore.

When their departure date finally arrived, the international atmosphere had reached a fever pitch. As Bogdan and Anastasiia left for the airport, a tense United Nations Security Council assembly was underway in Munich. Russian forces had massed at Ukraine's borders, enveloping significant stretches from the south, east, and even north via their presence in Belarus.

Still, many people in Kharkiv, including their relatives, believed that Putin was unlikely to follow through on his threats. While the couple could not shake off their apprehensions entirely, the reassuring sentiments of their loved ones made them downplay the risk. Filled with anticipation for their new chapter in Germany and the heartache of leaving their family behind, Anastasiia and Bogdan were excited to embark on this new adventure and planned to return in March to gather the belongings that they had temporarily left behind, as well as their cherished cat Rubik, who would be cared for by Anastasiia's family.

Named after the Rubik's cube, their feline companion had a sleek, glossy coat of midnight-black fur, reminiscent of a graceful panther. In soft lighting, this inky fur shimmered, revealing subtle undertones of brown and red. Rubik's eyes were a striking shade of mellow green, and his long, elegant whiskers twitched and quivered with every flicker of curiosity.

The instant they spotted him among his littermates, Anastasiia and Bogdan had fallen in love with Rubik's captivating personality. He was only three weeks old when his mother died. The couple lovingly bottle-fed him every four hours around the clock for several weeks until Rubik grew into a healthy, playful kitten. He was cheeky, always ready to chase elusive sunbeams that danced across the room. With age, he became more gentle and affectionate, mastering the art of finding the cosiest corners of their home. Come dusk, he would snuggle up close to them, purring contentedly as his plea for affectionate pats and ear scratches was heard. His presence brought a sense of tranquillity and comfort to their home; they knew they would miss him dearly.

While Bogdan's parents lived in Poland, Anastasiia's immediate family, comprising her parents and two younger brothers, resided in Kharkiv. They had all come to the airport to see the couple off. As they stood amidst the hustle and bustle of the departure hall, Anastasiia and Bogdan braced themselves for the impending goodbyes, their expressions a bittersweet mix of excitement and melancholy. Anastasiia's mother, Natalia, clung tightly to her daughter, holding back tears. Her father stepped forward, his stoic demeanour masking the whirlwind of emotions beneath.

He turned to Bogdan and said, 'Have a safe flight and take good care of my daughter. We'll see you in a few weeks.'

'I promise. We'll be back before you know it to collect Rubik and the rest of our belongings.'

Anastasiia's younger brothers embraced their sister firmly before they started walking towards the gates. At the entry to the security check, the couple paused, looking back and waving goodbye to their family one more time before they were out of sight.

Anastasiia and Bogdan boarded the aeroplane with an unsettling feeling. Germany had issued a storm warning, and weather alerts painted a bleak picture of Dortmund, their destination. Two storm systems, ominously named 'Ylenia' and 'Zeynep', were forecasted to unleash winds exceeding 150 km/h. Schools had been ordered to stay closed and households were in a frenetic rush to secure their properties, especially the vulnerable rooftops. At higher elevations, winds were expected to reach hurricane levels.

An hour into their flight, Anastasiia noticed the once-clear sky assuming a menacing hue. Torrential rain and a canopy of dark clouds obliterated visibility, making it almost impossible to identify anything but sinister silhouettes. A few minutes later, the aircraft started to sway and tilt in the winds outside. The turbulence forced the aeroplane into sudden and jarring movements, bouncing on each gust. She clung to the seat, holding Bogdan's hand tightly as they were pushed and pulled in different directions. The plane's core reverberated with unsettling vibrations, causing a steady and disorienting noise, while the wings, though sturdy, shook noticeably, struggling to withstand the now unpredictable currents of the storm.

The closer they got to Dortmund, the stronger the turbulence became. Anastasiia and Bogdan felt the aeroplane ascending and descending as the pilot adjusted altitude and course, making an effort to steer clear of the storm's wrath.

Anastasiia and Bogdan held each other's hands, their clenched knuckles turning white. Amidst the disconcerting symphony of noise and motion, they exchanged anxious glances. Anastasiia's voice almost got lost in the chaos as she gripped her seat tightly and murmured over the din, 'Bogdan, this feels much worse than normal turbulence.'

Bogdan, trying to keep his own fear in check for Anastasiia's sake, squeezed her hand gently. 'Not for much longer, Anastasiia. We're almost through it.'

'I hope so. It's so intense!' she whispered, her eyes darting towards the window where the night was lit intermittently by lightning.

Bogdan locked his gaze with hers. 'It's going to be okay. These planes are built to withstand much more than a storm.'

Both of them were drenched with sweat as they finally stepped off the aeroplane forty-five minutes later. Their feet shaky, they made their way to the airport shuttle after collecting their luggage. It would take them to Holzwickede, a small town only a five-minute ride away, where they would catch the regional train to their final destination. Yet less than thirty minutes into the train ride, their travel came to an abrupt halt.

'Due to severe weather conditions, our service terminates here today. All passengers, please disembark. We apologise for any inconvenience,' blared a voice over the loudspeaker.

Though they did not understand German, the collective grumbling of their fellow passengers signalled that something was amiss. As their neighbours began to exit, they explained that a taxi would be the couple's only option to reach their final destination. Anastasiia and Bogdan proceeded to the taxi rank just outside the train station, steeling themselves for what would turn out to be one of the most costly cab rides of their lives.

As they watched the wind blow over the snowy fields outside, Bogdan could not shake the foreboding feeling that the series of unfortunate events they had just experienced was a harbinger of dark days ahead.

Chapter 23

The guilt of the lucky

17–24 February 2022

The couple had arranged an apartment online for their initial month in the new town. They believed that four weeks would be ample time to secure a more permanent residence. The apartment was only a short drive from the train station. As their taxi pulled up, a welcoming woman with blonde hair reaching her shoulders greeted them from the entrance.

'You must be Anastasiia and Bogdan,' she began warmly. 'Welcome to Germany. Please come inside.'

She managed the apartment with her husband. The middle-aged German couple resided in the same building and was always keen to interact with the travellers and newcomers they hosted. They provided Anastasiia and Bogdan with tips, eager to help them settle in quickly.

One week later, on 24 February 2022, a groggy Bogdan reached for his phone from the bedside table. In an instant, alertness superseded his drowsiness as he processed the disturbing headlines. Beside him, Anastasiia too began scrolling, her face contorted with fear and disbelief. Bogdan turned to her, his eyes scanning the words again as if to confirm they were real.

'Nastya,' he whispered, his voice tight, 'Russia has invaded Ukraine. The news says there's fighting in Kyiv and Kharkiv.'

Anastasiia's heart raced as she stared at her own screen.

'We need to call our families. I'll call my parents. You get in touch with your uncle.'

As they reached out to their loved ones, messages poured in from Norway, where their former colleagues were well aware that they had returned home in December.

Bogdan and Anastasiia felt shocked, alarmed, and helpless. Had they foreseen this, they might never have departed. Now both their families found themselves trapped in Kharkiv, perilously close to the Russian border, where the fighting intensified by the minute.

Only a week prior, Anastasiia had tearfully bid her family farewell, anticipating a reunion in a few weeks. At this moment, all she could do was maintain contact by phone and track their every step. While Bogdan's parents resided in Poland, his grandmother was in Izyum, just over 120 kilometres southeast of Kharkiv, and his aunt, uncle, and cousin were based in the city. For them, the day of the invasion was nothing short of tormenting. Their initial impulse to evacuate by car on the morning of 24 February 2022 was swiftly quashed by the stark realisation that neither of their two vehicles was fit for refuge. One was electric, which meant they would inevitably get stranded within Ukrainian borders on their way west. The other required urgent repair.

Bogdan and Anastasiia tried to support their friends and family as best they could but their options from Germany were limited. Alongside countless other Ukrainians and global spectators witnessing the harrowing events, the overwhelming feeling of powerlessness threatened to pervade their every day. Minor acts provided a brief solace, such as arranging safe transportation for friends opting to leave Ukraine and enjoying moments of connection with their family, albeit confined to digital channels, or fundraising for Ukraine's army.

Much like the four of us on the Google Meet call, regular check-ins became part of their routine for the next few days. Reassurance of their loved ones' safety provided a beacon of hope every day. Conversely, periodic silence when infrastructure damages resulted in communication blackouts across Ukraine plunged them into agony. These lapses in communication made the days seem endless, their attention constantly drifting from one distraction to the next. Immersion in work offered some relief, yet focusing remained a challenge.

In rare moments when they could stave off the feelings of despair and grief over the injustice, one relentless emotion remained that was the hardest to silence: the guilt of the lucky. Their timely escape from the war zone was a fluke. The random pricing of a flight might have saved their lives. Why had they escaped when so many others had not?

DONETSK

Chapter 24

Erase my language, erode my identity

2 March 2022

It is Wednesday. As usual, I log on around 6am and find Olena already online. She looks terrified and devastated, and her eyes are red and swollen from crying. They speak volumes of her pain. Russian troops started shelling her town last Friday, cutting it off from electricity. Encircling it, they now keep it under siege and are facing heavy clashes with Ukraine's battalion day and night.

Olena's friends and their children have taken refuge in a bunker and have been without food or water for more than two days. Their once peaceful town life has been reduced to the bare essentials of survival. For the past two days, they have been roused from sleep by the unyielding chill and dampness of their subterranean shelter. Breakfast, meagre and rationed, is consumed under the wavering glow of candlelight, in quiet conversation with the children to preserve energy for the unforeseen challenges each new day brings. Unknown voices filter through the static of their battery-powered radio, providing updates on the situation outside, which remains grim. They fill the dragging hours with tales, songs and silent games—anything to distract the children from the gnawing sensations of hunger and thirst, the biting cold, and the dullness of confinement. Moments of reprieve are found in brief naps and fleeting chances to capture natural light and gulps of fresh air whenever the situation allows. The uncertainty makes each day unpredictable. As dusk falls, they huddle together for warmth in the pitch darkness, taking turns trying to catch a few hours of sleep while the others keep watch.

No one knows whether they will survive. Olena knows for sure that her town did not. Almost all of the buildings have been damaged or completely destroyed. By the time the siege ends, there will be nothing left.

She is originally from Volnovakha, a modest town with a population of little more than 20,000, situated seventy kilometres south of Donetsk, near the Russian border. Her husband Dmytro grew up in Kurakhove, a town of similar size located approximately fifty kilometres west of the city. For both of them, the fight for the survival of their homes started much earlier.

Russia began exerting its influence over this region of Ukraine decades before the invasion in February 2022, which finally drew the attention of the Western world. When Olena's parents were young adults, a Russian propaganda campaign was in full effect, aiming to reshape the perception of Ukrainian identity. Russian TV shows, which were widely broadcast throughout the country, portrayed Ukrainian characters as foolish, uneducated, and addicted to alcohol. By the time Olena's parents left their villages to attend university, they were compelled to abandon their native language in favour of Russian to be accepted. Identifying as Ukrainian took on a derogatory connotation, associated with the working class from rural areas, often with limited formal education, and being recognised as such could lead to severe social repercussions. To avoid ridicule, exclusion from communities, and other forms of social ostracism, many Ukrainians felt pressured to conceal their heritage. It became an unavoidable sacrifice in the pursuit of a better life. Ukrainian traditions gradually took on different associations, and the natural ways to pass them down from one generation to the next began to fade away.

About a decade later, as Olena and Dmytro were starting elementary school, Russian had firmly established itself as the dominant language in all facets of life. From public services to local grocery stores, navigating daily life required speaking Russian, and even Ukrainian surnames had been modified to erase traces of the language.

Olena and Dmytro learned Ukrainian as their second language, with all subjects, except for Ukrainian literature and language, being taught in Russian. Living sixty kilometres apart and being strangers to one another, both young Olena and Dmytro began to question why they were speaking Russian when their country had its own distinct language. Silently, they each harboured a desire to reclaim Ukrainian as their primary tongue. However, this was no small feat.

Olena had broached the subject with friends and romantic partners, only to be met with mockery and derision. She had almost become resigned to the painful possibility of never having a family that would speak Ukrainian and uphold Ukrainian traditions when she met Dmytro at the University in Donetsk. After noticing his pro-Ukrainian stance on social media, Olena mustered the courage to suggest making the switch back to Ukrainian. To her delight, Dmytro agreed.

The transition back to their native language was challenging. They frequently consulted dictionaries and painstakingly shifted from translating from Russian to thinking and dreaming in Ukrainian for the very first time in their lives. Finding strength in each other, they encouraged their parents and some friends to attempt the shift, too. While many tried, they found it daunting to maintain in their daily lives, and struggled with the lack of vocabulary and fluency.

By nurturing a generation that spoke exclusively Russian, Russia had effectively relegated the Ukrainian language—and, by extension, Ukrainian identity—in the region to a mere flicker. At the time, succumbing to the pressure to speak Russian might not have seemed as significant, but it would reverberate through future generations, leaving a legacy of guilt for permitting their neighbours to erode the nation's identity.

Chapter 25

The burden of injustice

27 February 2014–24 February 2022

Olena and Dmytro's lives took a dramatic turn in the spring of 2014 with Russia's annexation of Crimea and the ensuing war in Donbas. Following the ousting of President Viktor Yanukovych earlier in the year, pro-Russian separatists, backed by Russia, had declared the Donetsk People's Republic and seized control of various government buildings within the Donetsk and Luhansk regions in eastern Ukraine.

Only a year had passed since the couple had settled in Donetsk, following a two-year sojourn in Lviv. Olena's coffee shop was flourishing. She rose at dawn every day, preparing for the rush of regulars she knew by name, who eagerly sought their essential morning brew. Her shop was a cosy hub for locals, a place where the aroma of freshly ground coffee beans and oven-baked pastries filled the air. It provided a space for warm conversations during quieter moments of business, later yielding to the lively clatter of cups and customer chatter overpowering the gentle strains of music in the background. Dmytro pursued his own career in IT but regularly stopped by and sometimes helped her close the shop at the end of the day. Well-deserved days off were devoted to leisurely walks in Donetsk's lush parks, enjoying the city's vibrant cultural life, and catching up with friends. Life was tranquil, fulfilling, and overall content—truly a life well lived.

Within a few weeks, it all changed. As the conflict rapidly escalated, armed clashes, artillery bombardments, and civilian casualties became daily occurrences. Olena finally made the heart-wrenching decision to return to her hometown. On her final day in Donetsk, as she was shutting down her coffee shop, she could hear the sounds of the Russian military clashing with Ukrainian forces.

Olena and Dmytro initially sought refuge with her parents in Volnovakha. While Donetsk had fallen under Russian control, Volnovakha remained under Ukrainian authority, at least for the time being. Yet they were acutely aware that this state might not last. The residents of Donbas were condemned to exist in a liminal space for years to come, living 'normal' lives while simultaneously fighting for their sense of belonging and their right to remain part of their homeland. Eventually, her parents relocated further north, where her grandmother owned a house, while Olena and Dmytro made the decision to move to Germany. There, they built a family, welcoming three kids: their daughter Sophia, followed by twin girls.

In the early days of 2022, as the tension in Ukraine became palpable, the couple started to warn their friends about the impending peril. They were among the few who believed that Russia was plotting a large-scale attack across Ukraine. Their warnings were met with the inertia of disbelief that Russia would dare to transgress, especially in the western regions of Ukraine. This denial, it seemed, was the common refuge of their friends—a comfortable blind spot in the human psyche, far easier to inhabit than the unsettling acknowledgement of a looming crisis. The couple insisted, trying to puncture the bubble of normality their friends clung to, urging them to prepare for the gravity of events that were about to unfold.

The eve of 24 February 2022 was marred with unrest. The children's sleep was restless and kept Olena, drained and weary-eyed, awake most of the night. Long before dawn, Dmytro took over the care of the young ones, allowing her a fleeting moment of respite. As she gently opened the bedroom door at dawn, she found him, still and tense, at the kitchen table, his gaze immediately meeting hers.

'Have you seen the news?' he asked urgently, not pausing for her to respond before he continued. 'The war… It's begun. Ukraine is under fire.'

Words failed Olena. The air around her grew thin. Her first thought went to her three children. She had brought them into this world hoping it would be safer for them than it had been for her so far. She had dreamt of giving them a life where they would never witness the horrors she had in 2014, and would never have to question the sovereignty of their country or rise to its defence.

She shook her head in a desperate bid to break this train of thought that would take her to even darker places. Fingers trembling, she texted her parents. Their digital exchanges would span almost a week before she was able to hear their voices. She was afraid of crying, of crumbling under her emotions when strength was most required of her. After all, she was nestled in the safety of Germany, while her parents were engulfed in the chaos of a war zone.

Afraid of frightening the children, she suppressed her tears, retreated to the bedroom, and softly closed the door. She held on by a thread until Dmytro took the children to kindergarten. The moment the door clicked shut behind them, she burst into tears. She had been to this dark place before and wished so dearly never to find herself in this hell again.

'It's so unfair. So unfair,' she whispered to herself, her voice a fragile murmur. It was the sheer helplessness that struck her the hardest—the stark realisation that she was powerless to alter the course of events, to prevent the suffering, and to halt the relentless march of war. In this moment, she yearned to fade away into nothingness.

Yet, as the hours wore on, she somehow found herself connected to our company's task force call. Being amidst our voices brought her unexpected

The burden of injustice

solace. While we all felt powerless, we were powerless together. In our shared vulnerability, we carried each other through the day.

When the children returned from kindergarten, they immediately sensed the unspoken turmoil that hung heavy. Their instincts drew them closer to her, their bodies seeking solace in her presence. In an unprecedented need for comfort, they clung to her with a fervency that she had not witnessed before. Every attempt to put them down resulted in piercing cries.

In the night that followed, Olena did not close an eye. She navigated between the soft glow of her laptop screen and the quiet sanctuaries of her children's bedrooms. In the silence of the night, she watched over their peaceful slumber while she scrolled through the news, seeking answers and hope.

Her thoughts travelled back in time to her grandmother. In the very first video that her family ever recorded, her grandmother had recounted her own harrowing experiences during World War II.

'My dearest wish for you is to never witness the ravages of war. For you to never experience the hardship I've gone through, to never tremble in fear for your life. May you know nothing but peace,' her grandmother had said, her words laden with the weight of lived experience.

As a child, Olena had replayed the video countless times, yet the true essence of war, the complexity of emotions that surged when one's homeland was under attack, remained elusive. It was only in 2014, when Russia invaded, that she felt the full brunt of war's grim reality. Much like her grandmother, she had harboured the fervent wish for future generations to remain untouched, for her future children to live in peace.

It was the innocence and vulnerability of her children that prevented her from succumbing to the pain and staying in bed the next morning. For their sake, she mustered the strength to rise and to clothe and feed them. While her own future seemed shrouded in darkness, she had to forge a path forward to find light for theirs.

Chapter 26

Together, we'd be strong

25–26 February 2022

Sophia was not told directly about the war, but it was impossible to shield her from it. It permeated every facet of the family's life, from the omnipresent news screens throughout the city to the very heart of their home. On Friday, Sophia accidentally caught sight of demolished homes on Olena's phone screen. At just four years old, she already had a bigger heart than most. She felt the world around her deeply, and was attuned to the emotions of those around her. With a grace unique to her, she climbed onto Olena's lap, her little arms encircling her mother's neck in a tender embrace. Her golden curls cascaded down her back, with that one rebellious strand that always insisted on escaping from behind her ear. Her sage-green eyes, wide with concern, searched Olena's for answers.

'Mummy, why are all those houses broken?' she whispered, her voice a soft murmur filled with confusion.

Olena drew in a deep breath, feeling the magnitude of the question. She had rehearsed this conversation in her mind countless times, but now, as she looked into her daughter's trusting eyes, the words escaped her. How could she possibly convey the harsh complexities of war to her daughter, yet keep her child's innocent mind safe?

'My love,' she began gently, her hand tenderly caressing Sophia's cheek, 'sometimes people can't agree on things or find a way to talk them out. Those broken houses, they're in our Ukraine. We're having a disagreement with Russia, and because of that, some things are getting broken. But we have brave people defending our country, and you, my darling, are safe here.'

Sophia nestled closer, her young mind trying to make sense of her mother's words.

'But, Mummy, what about the people in those houses? Are they okay?' Her voice quivered with worry. Olena's heart ached as she saw the concern in her daughter's eyes.

'Some of them are okay, sweetheart, because they have left their homes to find safer places. But it's also true that some people are hurt, and that's very sad,' she spoke gently, choosing her words carefully.

'Can we do something to help them?'

Olena nodded, feeling a surge of pride for her compassionate daughter.

'Yes, we can. We can send things home that people might need, and there are organisations we can give money to that can help them as well. Would you like to do that with me?'

'Yes. I want to help. I don't want anyone to get hurt.'

Olena kissed the top of Sophia's head.

'We'll do everything we can to help, together.'

The next day, Sophia was tucked cosily into the backseat of a car, next to her dearest companion, Lenny, a friend since their earliest days in daycare. Lenny's parents had generously offered to look after her for the day, providing a respite from the war-torn atmosphere at home. Olena was deeply immersed in the support initiatives organised by our company, while

Dmytro collaborated intensively with friends on their own relief efforts. Lenny's parents planned to spend the day at the public pool to distract Sophia from the troubling news that Olena had shared with her the previous day. She was an avid swimmer, eagerly awaiting her swimming lessons every week, her eyes lighting up at the prospect of taking a plunge.

Barely a few streets into the drive, a detour sign altered their path. A sea of blue and yellow flooded the road ahead, signs of a demonstration protesting against Russia's invasion of Ukraine. The crowd, dressed in Ukraine's national colours, passionately waved banners and shouted slogans. Lenny's eyes grew wide with curiosity as he pressed his face against the car window to inspect them more closely.

'What's happening, Dad?' he inquired.

Before Lenny's father could respond, Sophia, her voice unexpectedly firm for a four-year-old, interjected.

'There's a war in my country, Lenny,' she said, turning to look at him with a seriousness that belied her age. 'They're protesting against Russia for invading Ukraine.'

That evening, after a day filled with play and laughter, Lenny's parents dropped off a tired Sophia. Barely able to keep her eyes open while Olena brushed her teeth, she was soon ready for bed. Olena decided to read her a comforting tale about a young adventurous girl on a bicycle journey, exploring the wonders of the world. She could not help but see so much of her own daughter in the story: the curiosity, the tenacity, and the gentle spirit. As she kissed Sophia good night and was about to turn off the light, Sophia's soft voice stopped her.

'Mummy, I've been thinking. There's an easy solution to stop the war. The world needs to unite and stand up against Russia. Together, we'd be strong.'

Olena's heart swelled with a mix of pride and sorrow, a bittersweet smile playing on her lips. In a matter of days, the war had thrust adult burdens onto her little girl's shoulders. Sophia was navigating grown-up worries with a child's pure heart, forced to wrestle with thoughts far too complex for her age. The realisation struck Olena profoundly: Sophia would have to grow up much quicker than other children. 'It's not fair,' she whispered to herself.

Chapter 27

Who are we?
The quest for restoration

29 February 2022

On Monday morning, Dmytro accompanied Sophia to her kindergarten while Olena stayed behind with the twins. She had become reclusive in the days since the invasion began, keeping the outside world at arm's length. Even a simple 'How are you doing?' felt like a jab, threatening to dismantle the fragile barricade she had constructed around her emotions, potentially leaving her in tears. Sophia's kindergarten was a leisurely fifteen-minute walk from their home. She cherished these moments, her small fingers securely entwined with her father's. To any passerby, it was just another ordinary Monday morning. The city's rhythmic pulse remained unchanged: buses honked, bicycles whizzed by, and people bustled, eager to kick-start their week. Only the replays on the news screens and the lampposts plastered with blue and yellow posters served as reminders of the weekend's demonstration.

Mid-journey, father and daughter made their customary stop at Dmytro's favourite coffee shop. These past few days had whittled down their time together, rendering these moments all the more precious. Dmytro ordered his usual cappuccino and encouraged Sophia to choose a treat for herself. As he lifted her to glimpse the pastry selection, he sensed her body tense in his arms. She clung to him, her grip on his neck so tight that it choked him momentarily.

'Dad,' she whispered, her voice tremulous, barely audible, 'I'm scared. I heard Russians. What if they attack us?'

Perplexed for a moment, Dmytro tightened his embrace, drawing his daughter even closer as he searched for the right words of comfort. Looking into her fearful eyes, he murmured, 'It's okay, Sophia. We're in Germany. The Russians here won't harm us. You're safe.'

Yet, the shadow of doubt lingered in Sophia's eyes, a haunting uncertainty that refused to be quelled easily. In the weeks that followed, Dmytro would have to reassure her each time they overheard Russian being spoken in public. It was a painful reminder of how deeply the echoes of war had already imprinted themselves on his young daughter's psyche.

While we were stuck in the tunnel of our 24/7 call, Olena and Dmytro made every effort to maintain some semblance of normality for their children, ensuring that they continued to attend kindergarten and daycare and adhering to their usual routines. Nevertheless, every waking moment was consumed by their involvement in anti-war initiatives. The grim reality of war seeped into their home, its disheartening impact evident in Sophia's changing behaviour.

In kindergarten, she told the other children about the war, prompting her concerned educators to gather the children and attempt to translate the complexities of war into terms a four-year-old might grasp. The characters in her imaginative stories began to shift; Ukrainian figures stood tall as heroes, while Russians loomed as the antagonists. Her mind was occupied with contingency plans should her family's home come under threat, intermingled with fantastical dreams of unicorns swooping in to rescue her homeland. Blue and yellow became her favourite colours, finding their way onto canvases she painted for friends and family. Her curiosity about

Ukrainian culture burgeoned. She peppered Olena with questions about traditional clothes, cuisine, and songs, revealing a growing desire to immerse herself in the rich tapestry of her heritage.

Both adults and children had to learn how to live with the war, and to navigate the two worlds they now lived in. In Germany, they experienced a semblance of normality, with days unfolding predictably. Yet on the screens of their phones, a different reality lurked—a world of urgent news flashes, harrowing images, and desperate social media posts about their homeland at war.

Their emotions were a roller coaster. Adapting to this new reality is no small feat. The relief of being away from the immediate danger was always tinged with palpable guilt. The plight of those enduring the war firsthand was unfathomable. Their thoughts constantly gravitated towards loved ones back home, some of whom lived in territories now occupied. Communication became a precarious dance, with words weighed carefully, tainted with the fear that a misplaced word could cause them trouble.

For Sophia, like thousands of other children, the war, in its relentless ferocity, will leave an indelible mark on her character. She is destined to grow up understanding the importance of standing up for one's country and its right to exist. She will learn that justice sometimes demands a fight, and that maintaining one's self is a right worth defending.

The war has begun to reshape her generation's perception of what it means to be Ukrainian. Gone is the caricature of a frivolous, inebriated man propagated by Russian media. In its stead, a renewed reverence for Ukrainian history, literature, and culture has emerged. For many of us who have not fully grasped Ukraine's distinct national identity over the past decades, being Ukrainian signifies nothing but strength, resilience, bravery, and an unwavering love for one's homeland. It is the mark of a nation's identity on the verge of rebirth.

Ironically, Putin might have inadvertently ignited the very opposite of what he intended: a nation rallying around an identity once perceived as fractured, now burgeoning with even greater vigour. And yet, the price for this restoration—the pain, the loss, and the anguish of stolen childhoods—is profoundly unjust.

Chapter 28

Grasping for the new normal

2 March 2022

Wednesday marks our last evening on a continuous call that has spanned seven relentless days and nights. In the dim glow of my computer screen, I reflect on the whirlwind of the past week. We have been a lifeline to our colleagues in Ukraine, navigating the tumult of the Russian invasion with little rest. As our company's makeshift task force, we have now established a Telegram channel to better coordinate our efforts—a small yet significant triumph in the face of the chaos of recent days.

We agree that it is time to take a break, but the decision to step back is fraught, considering that the world looks no better than it did seven days ago: our colleagues are on the front line, cities across Ukraine are battered by ceaseless shelling, and the refugee count has surged past 870,000. Our daily lives might be shifting, but the crisis we are entrenched in is not.

'We can use our work tool, Slack, or our Telegram channel for urgent communications,' Danylo suggests during the last minutes of our call.

'Sounds good. Let's get off this call and transition to daily check-ins instead,' we agree.

Olena, ever organised, volunteers to schedule these check-ins for 10am each day. So, for the first time in seven days, I press the 'leave call' button on Google Meet.

The next day brings a jarring dissonance. After a night of much-needed sleep, muscle memory leads me back into my routine of the past week: I brush my teeth, make a cup of tea, and sit down at my work desk in my pyjamas. After I unlock my laptop, Google Meet appears on my screen. Out of habit, I press 'join call'. No one's here. For a second, a brief surge of panic is rising inside me; did I miss something crucial? Damn, why did I sleep in? Then I recall that we agreed to daily task force calls instead of continuous Google Meet calls.

At 9.58am, I join the video call. It feels both alien and familiar. As I scan the faces on my screen, I realise that the comfort of routine, even a newly minted one, is invaluable. For now, the tasks at hand are manageable. Our Telegram channel is quiet—a rare pause in the relentless flow of updates.

In the days that follow, our focus pivots from immediate crisis response to longer-term solutions. We wrestle with the logistical nightmare of securing housing in Germany amidst a stark housing crisis, exacerbated by the influx of Ukrainians seeking refuge in Europe. Lesya's situation is particularly pressing—finding a space for several adults, four cats, and a dog is no small feat.

As more of our colleagues reach Germany, they collide with the wall of bureaucracy that guards the gates to a new life here. We expand our use of Notion, collating information vital for navigating these new waters. Many of the tasks are labyrinthine for those unfamiliar with German procedures. For example, it is obligatory to register at the relocation address within three days of arrival, apartment contracts are usually signed for at least one year with a three-month notice period to the end of the month, and support services for physical and mental health have started to surface, but accessing them still requires completing forms that are only available in English.

The transition from our online bubble back to a semblance of offline normality is difficult for me. The war raging on, indifferent to our changed routine, leaves me grappling with a pervasive sense of helplessness and grief.

Over time, this new reality seeps into my everyday life. I cling to small routines, seeking comfort in familiarity, yet the joy I once took from these simple pleasures is now tinged with sorrow I cannot seem to shake off. The dark cloud is ever-present.

Gradually, our meetings become less frequent, shifting from every other day to weekly as our roles demand that we return to more routine business tasks. Yet each meeting is a poignant reminder of the deep connections that we have forged under fire. It takes me straight back to the key moments of this week—jointly wrestling with our shock, withstanding eternal minutes of shelling, and suffering from worry as we face Ukraine under attack. In the course of seven days, we have evolved from co-workers to friends to family.

As we navigate this uncertain path forward, I realise that the true strength we have gained is not just in our ability to cope, but in our capacity to support one another. The war may have brought us to our knees, but it also made us stand together, more united than ever before. During the dark days of winter 2022, we found hope in each other. May you find people who bring the same light to your darkness.

Epilogue

By Olena

Two years after the full-scale invasion, I wish I could write about the victory of Ukraine, but reality is cruel.

2022 was a year that changed everything for me and millions of Ukrainians. Russia's full-scale invasion of Ukraine left deep scars on our hearts, in our consciousness, and on our land. Life split into "before" and "after." Although I had already felt the war in 2014 when I had to leave my occupied city through a checkpoint manned by armed invaders, the brutal full-scale invasion knocked the ground from under my feet, instilling a pain in my soul that just won't go away.

I have three children, and the thought that I brought them into a world of cruelty, fear, injustice, and danger terrified me. And it still does. Years pass, and the situation worsens: people are being exterminated, and cities are being wiped off the face of the earth.

I do not wish for other nations to experience this grief, this hatred for the enemy, which you thought you would never be capable of, this helplessness. Life is no longer complete, and the most frightening thing is realising that until the war ends, it is impossible to fully live through it. You are forced to relive it again and again every day because every day you see photos of fallen defenders, whose bright eyes will no longer see their children, parents, friends...

The unbearable realisation is that if it hurts me so much, what must those Ukrainians in the centre of the events, on the front lines, be experiencing, those who no longer receive responses from their loved ones. The horrors of war can be described long and vividly. It is frightening that the world is tired of news from Ukraine, that weapons are delayed, and the human resources of Ukrainians also have their limits. It is a historical time when it will be defined whether good or evil will prevail. The words of Lina Kostenko come to mind:

And horror, and blood, and death, and despair,
And the screech of a predatory horde,
A little grey man
Has wrought black calamity.

This is a beast of a vile breed,
Loch Ness of the cold Neva.
Where are you looking, people?!…
Today it's us, tomorrow it will be you.

І жах, і кров, і смерть, і відчай,
І клекіт хижої орди,
Маленький сірий чоловічок
Накоїв чорної біди.

Це звір огидної породи,
Лох-Несс холодної Неви.
Куди ж ви дивитесь, народи?!...
Сьогодні ми, а завтра – ви.

Dear all, let us not let these words come true!

By Lesya

Moin Moin, Dear Reader!

It's extremely hard to briefly describe my whole experience and feelings about what happened during the last two years, but I'll try.

After one month in Bukovel, I and my three cats fled to Germany and my family went back to Mykolaiv. For the next year, I was trying to start my new life, while watching my old life and my hometown being destroyed. Right now, it's already been more than two years that I have lived in Hamburg, and I finally enjoy my life here. It was hard to accept the reality, that I didn't know if I ever could go back to Ukraine, so now I live for the present. Hamburg reminds me of Mykolaiv a lot, and it feels like home here, but the only thing I'm missing is my family. Fortunately, later my family was able to flee Ukraine, too. However, they live thousands of kilometres apart from me, so we can see each other only once/twice a year, but they're safe, and I'm happy.

The last thing I would like to say to you is that there is always something good even in the worst situation. I can't change what happened and what is still happening, but at least I can make the best out of the situation and enjoy my new life.

By Svetlana

After much pain, bitterness, fear, anger, anxiety, helplessness .. you find a way to function. My heart is broken every day and will stay so even after the war is eventually over. Nurture the good in you, and always help where you are able to help. You have the right to own your feelings and to master them. Also, never give up. Do not give up on yourself, on people, on this incredibly controversial life. Glory and victory to Ukraine.

By Larissa

On the one hand, I can still remember it all so clearly and know exactly how I felt during that time. On the other hand, it also feels like it was ages ago. I have since changed employers and now work for a social lottery, but whenever I hear about the Ukraine war, I think back to the colleagues I was in contact with during that period: Are they doing well now? Are they in a safe place? Are their families and relatives okay? Sometimes, I also feel guilty because I am not doing anything proactive to help any more.

I have immense respect for people who manage situations like ours daily or whose job it is to help people in such emergencies. When you've studied business administration and work in the business world, the biggest stress triggers are failing to meet a project deadline or failing to reach the expected effect with a certain budget. Such worries now seem trivial to me, and the weeks described in the book have taught me that there can be much more stressful moments, for example, when you're under time pressure to find secure accommodations or escape routes for colleagues who are fleeing. The trust and hope placed in me at that moment were a hundred times more stressful than any other responsibility I had to carry until then.

That time really bonded us as a team. We got to know each other anew or better, as privately as possible, when we appeared in front of the camera in pyjamas early in the morning, just out of bed. I suddenly became familiar with the homes of all my colleagues, their partners, and roommates who occasionally scurried past in the background. When you're on calls 24/7 and managing a situation like ours, you no longer care whether you appear "professional" on camera. This creates closeness and cohesion. I believe this team will always hold a special place in my heart. If we ever lost contact and a team member was to contact me asking for a favour, I couldn't say no and would offer support.

By Farid

Since I left Ukraine, which is now about two years ago, I still watch about an hour of news and the latest developments about the war every day.

I felt so comfortable in Lviv that I probably would have never travelled to Asia and South America as I did after the war. Perhaps I am still searching for a place and the people that I got to know in Lviv. Restless, that is how I would describe myself since then. I previously appreciated life there and now value it even more.

I miss the beautiful historic old town, the climate, the mountains, the culture, and my friends. I have now reached a point where I will return despite the war.

I know that we will win.
Slava Ukraini.

By Stefanie

Throughout the journey of documenting these stories, I have learned that courage has many faces and bravery knows no age or gender. The resilience of the Ukrainian people has never ceased to inspire me. Their strength and determination in the face of unimaginable adversity have left an indelible mark on my heart.

When I began this project, I was warned that publishing it would be difficult because readers have 'moved on.' Indeed, when searching for a publisher, I was repeatedly told that books about Ukraine no longer sell. Part of me understands this sentiment. Continuously engaging with complex subjects like war takes an emotional toll.

I am part of a generation of Europeans who grew up in peace, embodying pacifism, never expecting war to return to our doorstep. Our understanding of war came solely from the harrowing tales of previous generations. While we were shocked in the beginning, it is astonishing to me how quickly we adapted to not one but two conflicts near our borders in 2024.

The men and women whose stories are told in this book have not been able to move on. Ukraine has not moved on. Unless we are willing to let democracy become a relic of the past, none of us can afford to move on. Sadly, living in peace is still–and today more so than for decades–a privilege.

So, I encourage you, ask you, and yes, beg you, dear reader, to re-engage. If you are lucky enough to live in peace, cherish your daily privilege, be proactive in safeguarding it, and stand with those who are fighting in their pursuit of justice.

Acknowledgements

Stefanie King

This book would not have been possible without the support of the following exceptional individuals: My parents, who instilled persistence, moral courage, and unwavering optimism in me. My siblings, who always believe in me. Maria and Andi, my most precious supporters and role models, demonstrating the importance of acting according to one's convictions. My partner, extended family, and friends, who never ceased to cheer me on and became my most avid pre-readers.

My deepest gratitude goes to the protagonists of the book who entrusted me with their personal stories.

Special thanks to those who enabled me to advance and realise this project: Lynne Hackles (mentor), Jaya Chatterjee (editor), Danylo Pavliuk (designer), and Yurii Dubrovskyi (designer).

Finally, I extend my heartfelt thanks to those who supported me through good and bad times, my daily life heroes, and the beloved beings who are no longer with us but whose memory continues to inspire me.

Photographic Credits

The photographs in this book are reproduced by permission and courtesy of the following owners:

Olena (Lesya) Humeniuk: Chapter 21 (Bukovel)

Elizabeth Panyushkina: Chapter 21 (Mykolayiv, Varvaryvsky Bridge)

Farid Peter Malyar: Chapter 8 (Carpathian mountains) and Chapter 16 (equipment)

All other photographs belong to Dr. Stefanie King.

About the author

Dr. Stefanie King is an Austrian-Australian Innovation and Change consultant with a professional background in management consulting and entrepreneurship. Born and raised in Austria, she has an educational foundation in Business Administration, International Economics, and Linguistics, acquired through studies in Austria, Italy, and the United States.

Throughout her career, Stefanie has led diverse teams across various industries, drawing on her extensive experience to navigate complex challenges. Her passion for travel and deep interest in foreign cultures have shaped her empathetic approach to listening to people's stories.

Stefanie's journey as a writer began in her teenage years. Her latest work focuses on sharing the poignant stories of her team during the first weeks of Russia's invasion of Ukraine in 2022, providing a platform for their voices and experiences.

Today, Stefanie continues to guide organisations through crises and document narratives that offer a first-hand perspective on change, trauma, and conflict.

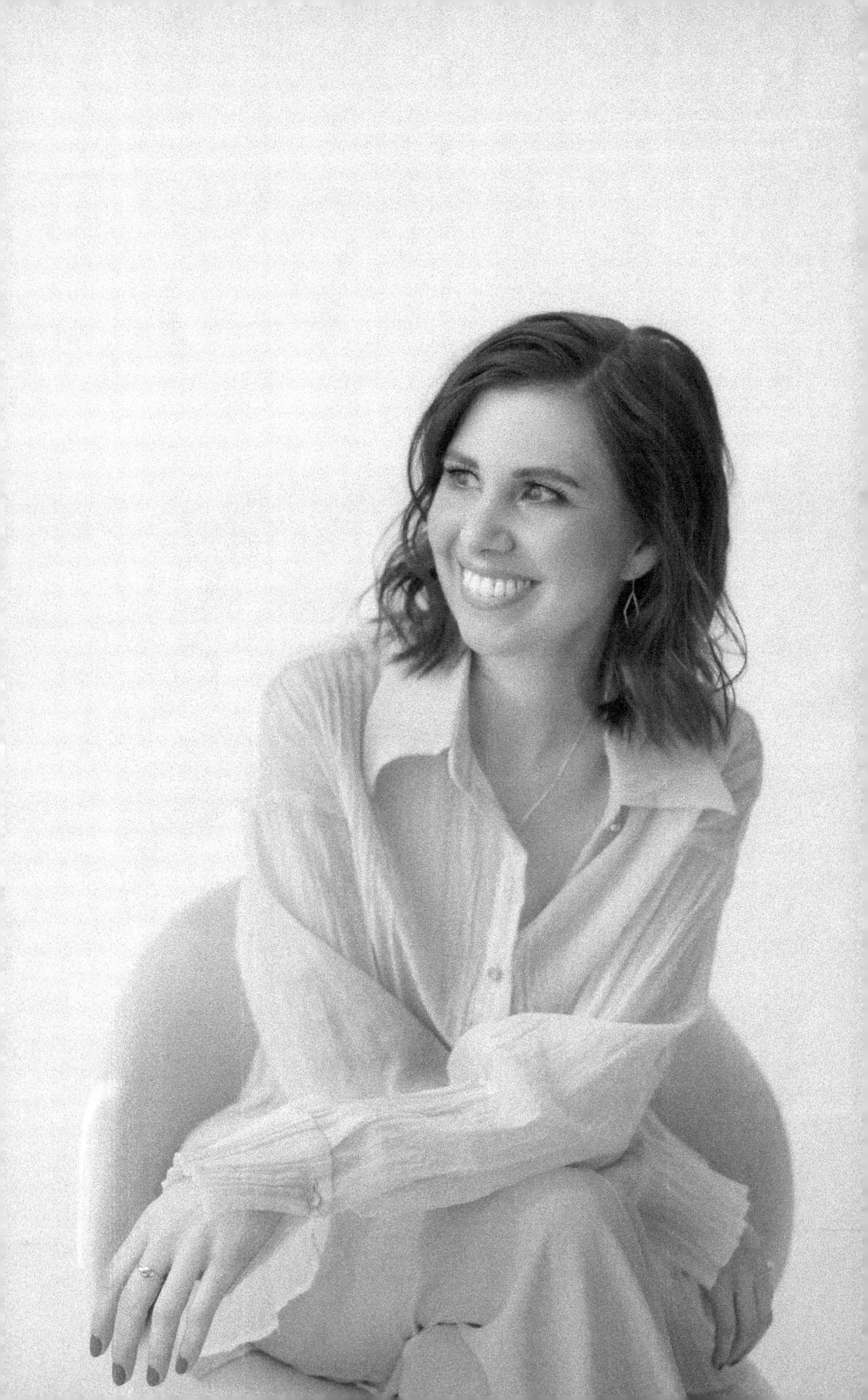

www.ingramcontent.com/pod-product-compliance
Ingram Content Group UK Ltd.
Pitfield, Milton Keynes, MK11 3LW, UK
UKHW030619050125
453011UK00002B/19